vtiger CRM
Beginner's Guide

Record and consolidate all your customer information with vtiger CRM

Ian D. Rossi

[PACKT] open source✳
community experience distilled
PUBLISHING
BIRMINGHAM - MUMBAI

vtiger CRM
Beginner's Guide

First published: July 2011

Production Reference: 1010711

Published by Packt Publishing Ltd.
32 Lincoln Road
Olton
Birmingham, B27 6PA, UK.

ISBN 978-1-84951-186-5

www.packtpub.com

Cover Image by Charwak A (charwak86@gmail.com)

Credits

Author
Ian D. Rossi

Reviewers
Thorsten Harbig

Alan Lord

Acquisition Editor
Robin de Jongh

Development Editor
Roger D'souza

Technical Editor
Pallavi Kachare

Project Coordinator
Michelle Quadros

Proofreader
Aaron Nash

Indexer
Tejal Daruwale

Production Coordinator
Aparna Bhagat

Cover Work
Aparna Bhagat

About the Author

Ian D. Rossi is an Internet business entrepreneur and passionate volunteer. His company, aimtheory, provides practical, on-target solutions to businesses utilizing the best in open source software. (See www.aimtheory.com for more information.) In the past Ian has provided technical solutions for the likes of Staples, Inc. and Intel. Ian also volunteers his time with a worldwide educational organization that helps people improve their lives. In 2007, Ian co-founded the hosted vtiger CRM service, aimtheoryCRM (www.aimtheoryCRM.com) and has served satisfied clients on every continent except for Antarctica.

I would like to thank my wife, Sheri, for her unending support and encouragement in writing this book.

About the Reviewers

Born on August 30, 1977, **Thorsten Harbig** grew up at the Lake of Constance in Southern Germany. He studied computer science, spent seven months in Belgium working on his Diploma Thesis and finished his Master's degree about energy savings on mobile phones at the Aalborg University in Denmark.

In 2006, Thorsten started working for LogicLine, a software consulting company in Sindelfingen near Stuttgart (Germany). In his daily work, he is a Java software architect for an internationally-active corporation in the automotive industry. He is always looking for new interesting topics to work on and to share new achievements with colleagues and others who are interested.

Alan Lord has over 20 years' experience in the IT industry. He has worked for companies that were some of the pioneers of the early Internet through to global telecommunications vendors.

For the last 10 years or so Alan has been building and running Linux systems both for business and pleasure. Around four years ago he co-founded the Open Source consulting company, Libertus Solutions (`libertus.co.uk`), to offer expertise and advice on Free and Open Source Software to businesses and public-sector organizations alike.

As well as being a business-minded Free Software evangelist, Alan's specialist expertise includes Ubuntu Linux and several open source applications including vtiger, OpenERP, Joomla, and Alfresco.

Alan writes a blog at `http://theopensourcerer.com` and can also be found on twitter @opensourcerer.

www.PacktPub.com

Support files, eBooks, discount offers, and more

You might want to visit www.PacktPub.com for support files and downloads related to your book.

Did you know that Packt offers eBook versions of every book published, with PDF and ePub files available? You can upgrade to the eBook version at www.PacktPub.com and as a print book customer, you are entitled to a discount on the eBook copy. Get in touch with us at service@packtpub.com for more details.

At www.PacktPub.com, you can also read a collection of free technical articles, sign up for a range of free newsletters and receive exclusive discounts and offers on Packt books and eBooks.

http://PacktLib.PacktPub.com

Do you need instant solutions to your IT questions? PacktLib is Packt's online digital book library. Here, you can access, read and search across Packt's entire library of books.

Why Subscribe?

◆ Fully searchable across every book published by Packt

◆ Copy and paste, print and bookmark content

◆ On demand and accessible via web browser

Free Access for Packt account holders

If you have an account with Packt at www.PacktPub.com, you can use this to access PacktLib today and view nine entirely free books. Simply use your login credentials for immediate access.

Table of Contents

Preface

Tap into the power of the free and open source software package, vtiger CRM—the popular alternative to commercial CRM tools. This powerful tool has enjoyed worldwide success and is being utilized by small and large organizations alike. You, too, can add real, modern CRM (customer relationship management) to your business model, and enjoy the growth that comes with it.

What this book covers

Chapter 1, Hello Kitty—What is vtiger CRM? introduces you to vtiger CRM and you'll learn a bit about its origin and history. The major technologies that make up vtiger CRM are outlined and the core feature set is explained.

Chapter 2, Unleashing the Beast—Installing vtiger shows you how to install vtiger CRM on a Windows or Linux system whether in the cloud or on a traditional server or computer.

Chapter 3, And the Claws Come Out—Getting Started With vtiger helps you to put vtiger CRM right to work. You'll import leads and/or customer accounts and create user accounts for your team. You'll also configure e-mail notifications and backup.

Chapter 4, Leashing the Beast—Using vtiger takes you on a tour of the vtiger user interface and show you how to effectively manage lists of CRM data. You'll also see how easy it is to track important customer data by cross-linking, storing documents and managing customer related e-mails.

Chapter 5, House Training your Secret Weapon—vtiger CRM and your Business shows you how to use vtiger CRM for your specific business model. You'll learn how to install custom modules, create custom fields and change the layout of the screen to suit your unique business model.

Chapter 6, Business Processes—They're G-r-r-r-reat! shows you how to implement your business processes with vtiger CRM. It will cover mapping custom fields and using workflows to support your sales and business processes.

Chapter 7, Super Tiger—Using vtiger Extensions helps you to see the power of vtiger extensions and how to use them. You'll be introduced to some of the most useful vtiger CRM extensions in the vtiger community.

Chapter 8, Facing the Tiger—vtiger Theming shows you how to customize the look and feel of the vtiger interface by creating your own custom vtiger theme.

Chapter 9, Kitty, Play Nice!—Integrating vtiger takes your external systems, such as your website, and integrates them with vtiger CRM using vtiger's API and vtiger's Web Lead Form.

Chapter 10, From Cub to King—Growing with vtiger shows you how to create your own custom module with the help of vtiger's vtlib module generation tool. You'll see how to also integrate your custom module with the other critical CRM data in vtiger CRM.

Appendix A: King of the Jungle—The Key to CRM Success is a bonus chapter that briefly outlines some important principles that will help you to make your CRM project a success.

What you need for this book

◆ To install and use vtiger CRM you will need access to a computer, server or cloud server running either Windows or Linux

◆ Internet access

◆ Some working knowledge of PHP and MySQL will be helpful, but not necessary

Who this book is for

◆ IT professionals

◆ CRM project managers

◆ Small business owners/operators

◆ Sales consultants

Conventions

In this book, you will find several headings appearing frequently.

To give clear instructions of how to complete a procedure or task, we use:

Time for action – heading

Action 1

Action 2

Action 3

Instructions often need some extra explanation so that they make sense, so they are followed with:

What just happened?

This heading explains the working of tasks or instructions that you have just completed.

You will also find some other learning aids in the book, including:

Pop quiz – heading

These are short multiple choice questions intended to help you test your own understanding.

Have a go hero – heading

These set practical challenges and give you ideas for experimenting with what you have learned.

You will also find a number of styles of text that distinguish between different kinds of information. Here are some examples of these styles, and an explanation of their meaning.

Code words in text are shown as follows: "We can include other contexts through the use of the `include` directive."

A block of code is set as follows:

```
deb http://security.ubuntu.com/ubuntu maverick-security main
restricted multiverse

deb-src http://security.ubuntu.com/ubuntu maverick-security main
restricted multiverse
```

New terms and **important words** are shown in bold. Words that you see on the screen, in menus or dialog boxes for example, appear in the text like this: "You can click on the **Convert Lead** link while viewing a lead to convert into a **Potential** and/or **Account**.

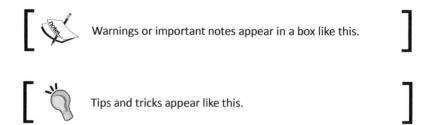

Warnings or important notes appear in a box like this.

Tips and tricks appear like this.

Reader feedback

Feedback from our readers is always welcome. Let us know what you think about this book—what you liked or may have disliked. Reader feedback is important for us to develop titles that you really get the most out of.

To send us general feedback, simply send an e-mail to feedback@packtpub.com, and mention the book title via the subject of your message.

If there is a book that you need and would like to see us publish, please send us a note in the **SUGGEST A TITLE** form on www.packtpub.com or e-mail suggest@packtpub.com.

If there is a topic that you have expertise in and you are interested in either writing or contributing to a book, see our author guide on www.packtpub.com/authors.

Customer support

Now that you are the proud owner of a Packt book, we have a number of things to help you to get the most from your purchase.

Downloading the example code for this book

You can download the example code files for all Packt books you have purchased from your account at http://www.PacktPub.com. If you purchased this book elsewhere, you can visit http://www.PacktPub.com/support and register to have the files e-mailed directly to you.

Errata

Although we have taken every care to ensure the accuracy of our content, mistakes do happen. If you find a mistake in one of our books—maybe a mistake in the text or the code—we would be grateful if you would report this to us. By doing so, you can save other readers from frustration and help us improve subsequent versions of this book. If you find any errata, please report them by visiting http://www.packtpub.com/support, selecting your book, clicking on the **errata submission form** link, and entering the details of your errata. Once your errata are verified, your submission will be accepted and the errata will be uploaded on our website, or added to any list of existing errata, under the Errata section of that title. Any existing errata can be viewed by selecting your title from http://www.packtpub.com/support.

Piracy

Piracy of copyright material on the Internet is an ongoing problem across all media. At Packt, we take the protection of our copyright and licenses very seriously. If you come across any illegal copies of our works, in any form, on the Internet, please provide us with the location address or website name immediately so that we can pursue a remedy.

Please contact us at copyright@packtpub.com with a link to the suspected pirated material.

We appreciate your help in protecting our authors, and our ability to bring you valuable content.

Questions

You can contact us at questions@packtpub.com if you are having a problem with any aspect of the book, and we will do our best to address it.

1

Hello Kitty—What is vtiger CRM?

Customer. Relationship. Management. These three words by themselves are enough to give us all nightmares, never mind all three of them together in the same sentence. But vtiger CRM takes the pain away and provides us with a solution that will leave us whistling the 1812 Overture (Yeah, you can make the cannon noises if you want). vtiger CRM is an open source customer relationship management tool written in the PHP scripting language, and it uses MySQL as its database. In this chapter you will learn about the CRM basics, the various components that make up vtiger CRM and its technical architecture. You will start to see the true potential of vtiger CRM through a brief discussion of customization potential.

In this chapter we shall:

- ◆ Take a quick look at the history of vtiger CRM
- ◆ Investigate the technical components of vtiger CRM:
  - ❑ PHP
  - ❑ Apache
  - ❑ MySQL
  - ❑ Smarty
  - ❑ CSS
- ◆ Review vtiger CRM's out-of-the-box, core CRM feature set
- ◆ Review vtiger CRM's potential for customization

The history of vtiger CRM

As you may already know, vtiger CRM is a fork of another CRM package called SugarCRM. SugarCRM was originally released under the SPL or "SugarCRM Public License". It's a modified version of the Mozilla Public License 1.1.

In 2004, Sridhar Vembu, CEO of AdventNet, created vtiger. SugarCRM was starting to "close" some of its source code for commercial gain. Vembu and the vtiger team created vtiger under the "honest open source" label based on SugarCRM's own SPL.

SugarCRM was openly upset by this movement. They called vtiger CRM "a lie" and claimed they were not living up to "the spirit" of open source. However, the vtiger team claimed full compliance with the SPL and openly admitted that it was a fork. They also sent a letter to Eric Raymond, a well-renowned advocate of open source. You can read the whole thread from 2004 at this URL: `http://forums.vtiger.com/viewtopic.php?t=11`. It's a very interesting read.

vtiger CRM states that they will protect the CRM to stay free with no dual versioning. Until now, vtiger has remained 100 percent open source and free. With the current version of vtiger—version 5—vtiger has lost almost all SugarCRM code.

The technical components of vtiger CRM

vtiger CRM is built on Apache, PHP, and MySQL. We'll review briefly each of these components below. Installation details follow in the next chapter.

Apache

Apache is another open source software project. Apache is a web server. A web server allows you to "host" a website. When you browse the Internet, Apache is what sends the content you're viewing to your screen. Of the roughly 255 million websites that existed in 2010, Apache hosted about 152 million of them.

vtiger CRM uses the Apache web server by default, although it can be configured to work with other web servers.

Make sure you have a working installation of Apache 2.0.40 or above. Little experience with Apache is necessary for the use of vtiger.

PHP

PHP is another open source software project. It is a sophisticated scripting language that benefits from the contribution of developers all over the world. PHP allows you to process data among many other things.

vtiger CRM is built on PHP. Over the last decade, PHP has become the scripting language of choice for many open-source and commercially hosted software packages. With vtiger CRM 5.2, PHP 5.3.x is recommended. If you have significant experience in PHP, you will have more potential for automation and more power in customizing vtiger CRM for your organization's needs.

MySQL

MySQL is a free, open source database management engine. It allows you to store, process, and retrieve relational data. vtiger CRM uses MySQL to store all of its CRM data.

To run vtiger well, MySQL 5.1.x is recommended. Like PHP, significant MySQL skill will unlock the true potential for customization that vtiger has.

Smarty

Smarty is a template engine designed for PHP. The result it that it separates the application logic (PHP) from the presentation or what you see on the screen. vtiger CRM uses Smarty to display its data, such as leads, accounts, and contacts.

You don't have to worry about installing Smarty or its version, as it installs along with vtiger. Smarty is a PHP-based templating system that allows vtiger to create its various views and layouts and merge them with vtiger's data layer, MySQL.

CSS

CSS (Cascading Style Sheets) is the standard by which colors and background images are applied in vtiger. If you are proficient in CSS, you can significantly change the look and feel of vtiger CRM and even make important usability improvements specific to your organization.

So, if you have experience with Apache, PHP, MySQL, and CSS, vtiger is a perfect fit for you and your organization. I'm sure you're eager to dig right in and start installing, but first let's take a look at vtiger's CRM feature set. Then you'll get a good picture of what you have to start with.

vtiger's core feature set

Lead Management, Sales Force Automation, Activity Management, and Customer Service are at the core of vtiger. However, there are plenty of other features that extend this core. There are also billing, inventory, email integration, and calendaring features that really start to build out the full-featured CRM that vtiger is.

There won't be an extensive consideration of all of vtiger's features in this chapter, but we'll get an overview of the core features that have to do with sales force automation. Later in the book we will get into more detail regarding each feature.

Sales and marketing features

First, here are some brief definitions of the terms that vtiger CRM uses. A **Lead** represents a company or a representative of a company that may have an interest in your products or services. A **Potential** is a lead that does have an interest in your products or services. An **Account** is either a customer or a prospect that has an attached **Potential**. A **Contact** is a person that is connected to an **Account**.

Multi-channel lead and account management is an integral part of CRM and is firmly supported by vtiger. You can capture leads from your website, enter them after a conference, etc. and vtiger will help you work on those leads and track them until they become business opportunities and then paying accounts.

Notice the default view of leads in the following screenshot. You can filter the lead view with custom filters so you can have visibility to specific segments of your lead pool, such as location, number of employees, revenue, sales stage, and so on:

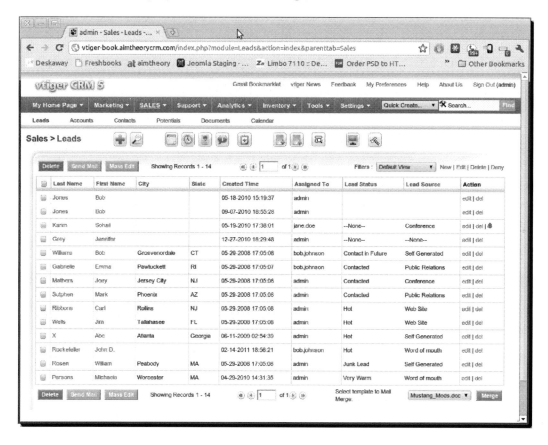

vtiger CRM also features an easy and secure web lead form (see Chapter 10 for more) that you can place on any website and it will insert new leads directly into your vtiger CRM system.

The lead details screen tells you everything you need to know about the lead on one page:

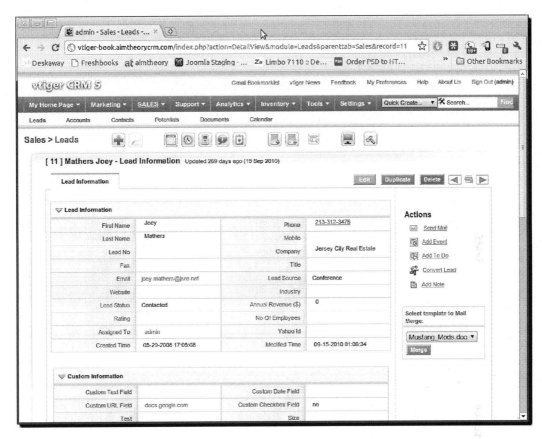

You can also incorporate a product-based selling process at the lead stage with integrated products. You can indicate any products that the lead is interested in.

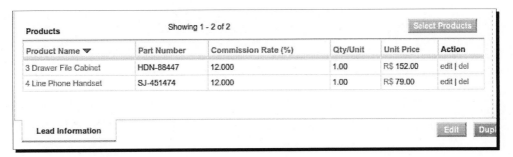

Once you have identified a lead as having potential for business, you can click on the **Convert Lead** link while viewing a lead to convert into a **Potential** and/or **Account**. We'll get into more detailed information about how to manage your sales process in vtiger CRM, but for now, you can see the power of vtiger CRM beginning to unfold and what it means for your sales process.

Activity management

vtiger CRM allows your team to manage their appointments on a shared calendar as well as schedule and assign tasks:

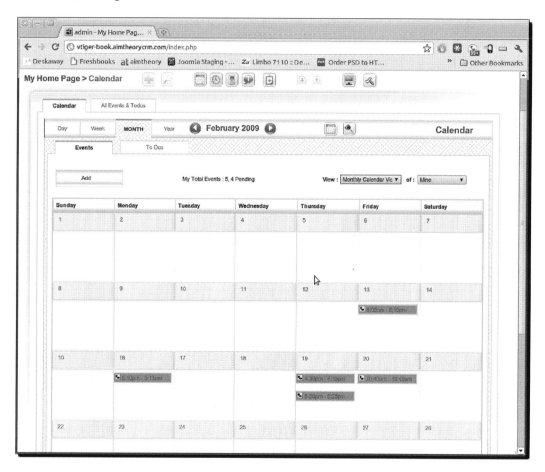

You can choose to see your appointments on a calendar view or you can look at them in list fashion if you prefer. With extensions, you can synchronize this with Microsoft Outlook and perhaps in the near future, with Mozilla Thunderbird.

Customer service/support

Of course, a critical piece of CRM is customer service/support. Full support for this is built into vtiger. Two features in particular contribute to a successful customer relationship: email management and ticket management.

E-mail management

Have you ever tried to find all of the emails regarding one client in Microsoft Outlook? It's a ridiculous endeavor unless you use folders, and even that can be more work than it's worth. vtiger CRM has a nice feature where you can send emails directly from the CRM and they'll be recorded in the lead/account details. There is even a mail converter available in the vtiger Extensions Marketplace that will scan an inbox for emails and match the recipient email addresses to your current leads/accounts and automatically attach them.

Email		Showing 1 - 2 of 2				Add Email
Subject	Related To	Date Sent ▼	Assigned To	Access Count	Action	
Initial Sales Meeting Invitation	Nunez Maria	06-18-2010	admin	0	edit | del	
Sales Meeting Follow Up	Nunez Maria	06-18-2010	admin	0	edit | del	

Ticket management

Resolving customer questions and issues is also a key to CRM success. Therefore, vtiger CRM features a **trouble ticket** module that provides full help desk or call center functionality. There is also an optional customer portal module that will allow your customers to login, create support requests, and view their status. This portal also shares much more information with the customer (see Chapter 7).

▽ Ticket Information

Ticket No	TT3	Assigned To	admin
Account Name	ABC Company	Priority	High
Product Name		Severity	Major
Status	Open	Hours	
Category	Big Problem	Days	
Created Time	05-18-2010 04:04:53	Modified Time	05-18-2010 04:06:04
Title	This is a pretty big problem. Please estimate and fix.		

Reporting

While vtiger CRM features canned reports, it also features a very powerful custom reporting tool that allows you to slice and dice your CRM data. And if you're good with MySQL, you can take that to the next level.

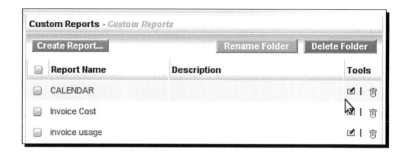

There is also a dashboard feature which uses visualizations to show data. These dashboards are all canned, but can be customized with some PHP and MySQL knowledge. Some dashboards are also featured on the home page.

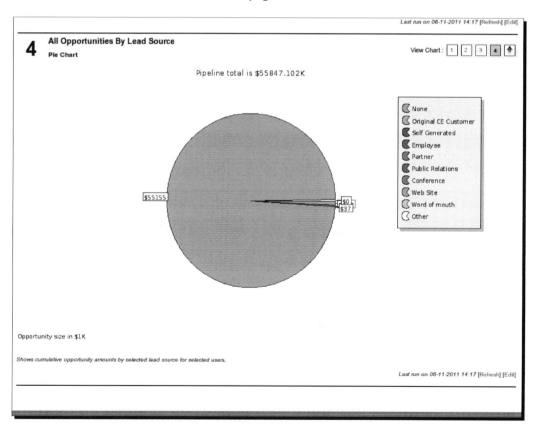

Document management

Sales people love attachments. Well, at least it seems like they do. Did you ever get an email from a sales rep and there are about 12 PDF's attached? vtiger tries to make their life a little easier by incorporating document management. Any user who is given access can create their own folders and upload any file type for storage on the vtiger server. They can even attach documents to outgoing emails to customers. This can help with document versioning and unify a sales team's efforts.

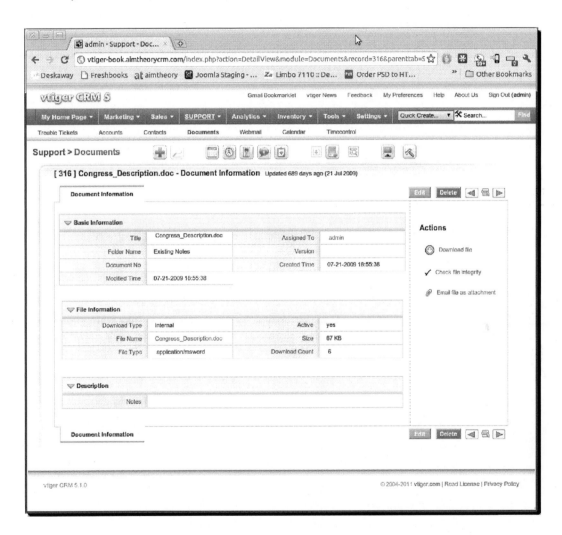

Pop quiz—What is vtiger CRM?

1. From where did vtiger CRM come into existence?
   a. Former disgruntled Sugar CRM employees
   b. Tony the Tiger
   c. An independent team of developers
   d. A tigon and a velociraptor

2. vtiger CRM is built with:
   a. PHP
   b. MySQL
   c. Both of the above
   d. Legos

3. vtiger CRM has the following features:
   a. Sales force automation
   b. Lead management
   c. Email integration
   d. All of the above
   e. A shiny utility belt

Summary

In this chapter we explored vtiger—its history, its technical architecture, and its core feature set. We discovered that vtiger offers powerful enterprise CRM features and the potential for customization.

We specifically learned:

◆ vtiger was originally forked from SugarCRM
◆ vtiger now has almost no SugarCRM code left
◆ vtiger's scripting language is PHP
◆ vtiger uses Smarty for HTML templating
◆ vtiger uses MySQL for its database
◆ vtiger uses CSS for layout and styling
◆ vtiger has a core feature set related to sales force automation

Now that we have taken a glimpse at the power of vtiger CRM and understood its potential, let's open the cage and let the cat out into the wild. In the next chapter, we'll create our own instance of vtiger CRM by installing it on our own computer or server.

2
Unleashing the Beast—Installing vtiger

In the early days of vtiger, installation was a deal breaker. Even IT pros would wipe the tears from their eyes as they ran to SugarCRM after fighting with the installation process. Since then, the vtiger CRM team has managed to "tame" vtiger during uncaging. Installation is now much easier. This chapter will guide you through a successful installation of vtiger CRM step-by-step.

In this chapter we shall:

- ◆ Install vtiger CRM on a Windows host:
    - ❑ Consider the system requirements for vtiger on Windows
    - ❑ Download and install vtiger on a Windows host
- ◆ Install vtiger CRM on a Linux host:
    - ❑ Consider the system requirements for vtiger on Linux
    - ❑ Download and install vtiger on a Linux host

So let's get on with it...

Installation on Windows

Before we begin the installation, let's consider the system requirements briefly.

System requirements

These are the same requirements that are listed on the website `www.vtiger.com`.

◆ **Hardware minimum**: Will run on a PC with at least an x486 Pentium 4 with 256 MB RAM and 200 MB free disk space.

◆ **Hardware Recommended**: x486 Pentium 4 with 512 MB RAM and 500 MB free disk space. (I would recommend more than this, at least 1 GB, especially if you'll be storing documents.).

◆ **Web Browser**: Firefox 2.x and above, Internet Explorer 6 and 7 (Google Chrome also works nicely).

◆ **Operating system**: Windows XP, 2003, Vista (Also works on Windows 7).

Installation prerequisites

The following is also listed on the website `www.vtiger.com`:

◆ You must have "Administrator privileges" on the system. If you are installing without Administrator privileges, vtiger CRM software will not be installed properly.

◆ Before installing vtiger CRM software, stop the Apache and MySQL services.

◆ vtiger CRM software is compatible with Apache 2.0.40, MySQL 5.1.x and above, and PHP 5.0.x and above.

Using the Windows installer

You may be brand new to web-based software and have a fresh, untouched Windows system that you want to use to host vtiger. The vtiger CRM team has prepared a special installer just for you. It packages Apache, PHP, and MySQL and installs them all at the same time as it installs vtiger CRM. Let's install it!

Time for action – Windows installation with the installer

1. Download the `vtigercrm-5.2.1.exe` from `http://sourceforge.net/ projects/vtigercrm/files/vtiger%20CRM%205.2.1/Core%20Product/ vtigercrm-5.2.1.exe/download` (or the latest release of vtiger).

2. Now save this file and run it.

3. The installation process will start with the **Welcome page**; click **Next** to continue with the installation:

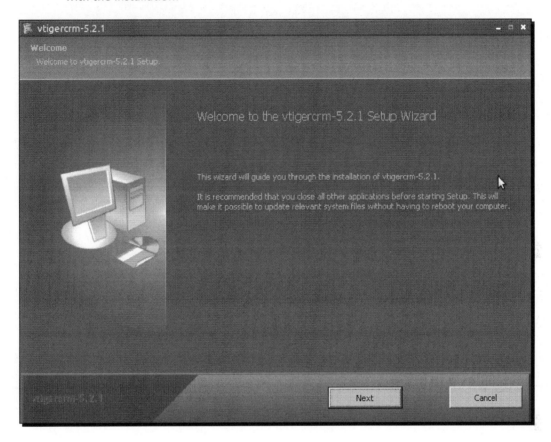

4. Next, you'll see the **license Agreement page**. You may choose whether to read it. Either way, click the **I accept** checkbox and click on **Next**:

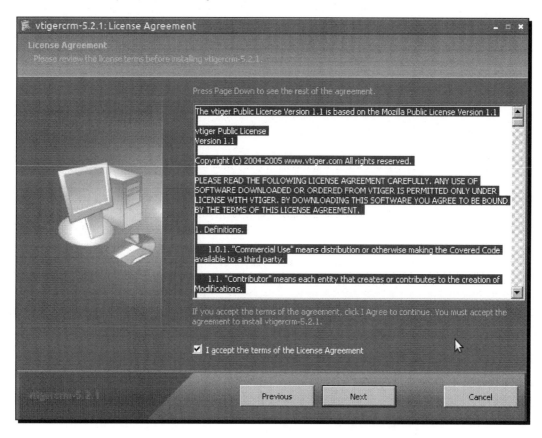

5. Now you're on the **Apache and MySQL Configuration Parameters** page. By default, the apache port is **8888**. If the port is occupied by any other process it will show a message saying this port is not free. Then you'll need to select a different port. You also have to provide the MySQL port, user name, and password. By default the MySQL port is **33307**. If the port is occupied by any other process it will show a message saying this port is not free, so you'll have to choose a different port. The default user name is root and the password is empty, you can change them to whatever you want. Then click on **Next**:

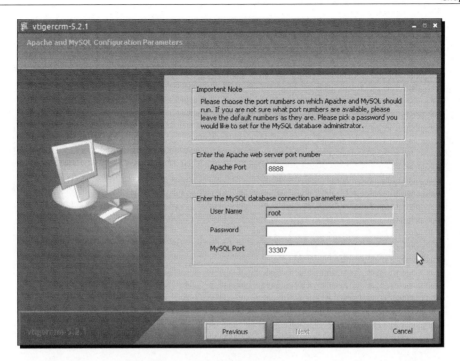

6. Now we are on the **User and Currency Configuration** screen. Here choose a password for the admin account, indicate the admin email address, and choose the primary currency to be used in vtiger CRM:

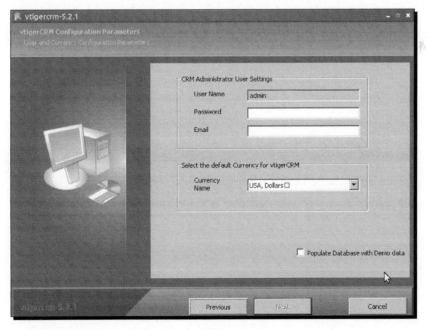

7. This brings us to the **Choose Install Location** page. Here you can select the installation directory. By default it's `c:\program files\vtigercrm-5.2.1`:

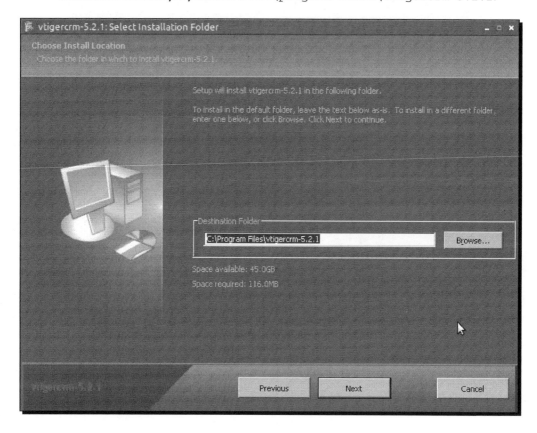

8. Click on **Next** again and this brings us to the Select **Start Menu Folder** page. Select the checkbox if you don't want to create a start menu folder. Now click on the **Install** button:

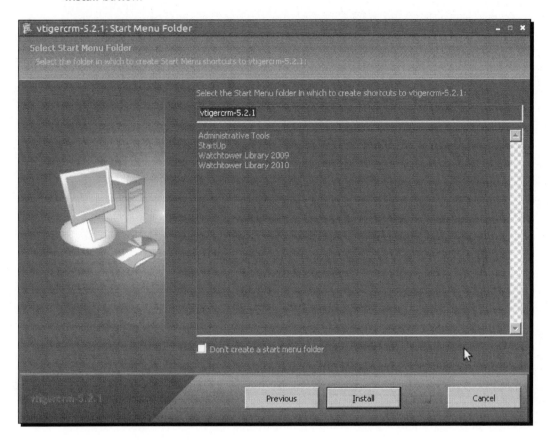

9. You have started the installation process. When the installation is done it will start the vtigercrm server, and it will launch a command window.

10. Now that vtiger is installed and started, you can skip to the section: *Using the Configuration Wizard*.

What just happened?

We just installed vtiger CRM on a Windows computer or server using the prepackaged Windows installer. We follow the steps in the installation wizard to set up Apache web server, the PHP scripting language, and the MySQL database engine.

Installing vtiger on Windows from source

This section is for those of you who are more technically savvy and are already familiar with Apache, MySQL, and PHP. It also assumes that you have a WAMP stack already configured. If you don't have this experience, stick with the Windows installer mentioned in the previous section.

For those who already have a Windows-based web server environment already configured with Apache, PHP, and MySQL, you'll want to install vtiger from source. In this section we'll do just that. You can also look up for a piece of software called XAMPP on Sourceforge (http://sourceforge.net/projects/xampp/) and install that. You can alternatively install any WAMP stack that you like. A WAMP stack is for Windows and includes Apache, MySQL, and PHP and other helpful pieces of open source software.

The steps below assume that you are familiar with administering Apache, PHP, and MySQL.

System requirements

First, briefly consider the system requirements:

◆ **Hardware**: Intel x86 with 512 MB RAM or more and at least 250 MB of disk space

◆ **Web browser**: Firefox 2.x and above, Internet Explorer 6 and 7

◆ **Web server**: Apache version 2.0.40 or higher or Microsoft IIS 5 or higher

◆ **Database**: MySQL version 4.1.x through 5.1.x

◆ **PHP**: version 5.0.x through 5.2.x

Time for action – Windows installation from source

Before grabbing the source code and unzipping it, let's make sure the system is configured properly:

1. First, enable the following extensions for your PHP setup:

GD	Mandatory	Charts and graphs generation are dependent on this library
IMAP	Mandatory	Webmails Module is dependent on this library
Zlib	Mandatory	For compression
OpenSSL	Optional	Imap with OpenSSL should be enabled in case Mail server needs to be connected via SSL
Curl	Optional	Needed for data transfer

2. Make sure to verify that your PHP configuration file (php.ini) meets the recommended values:

Variable	Value
zend.ze1_compatibility_mode	off
allow_call_time_reference	on
error_reporting	E_WARNING & ~E_NOTICE
safe_mode	off
display_errors	on
file_uploads	on
max_execution_time	600
memory_limit	32M
log_errors	off
output_buffering	on
register_globals	off
short_open_tag	On

3. Now download the vtiger CRM 5.2.1 source code (or the latest version). You can get 5.2.1 here: http://downloads.sourceforge.net/project/vtigercrm/vtiger%20CRM%205.2.1/Core%20Product/vtigercrm-5.2.1.tar.gz.

4. Now extract the downloaded file into your root web directory on Apache. Since it is a tar.gz file, you will need a Windows program that can extract them, such as 7zip.

5. Now provide read and write access to the web server user for the following files and folders and all of their subdirectories:

- ❑ config.inc.php
- ❑ tabdata.php
- ❑ install.php
- ❑ parent_tabdata.php
- ❑ cache
- ❑ cache/images/
- ❑ cache/import/
- ❑ storage/
- ❑ install/

- ❑ `user_privileges/`
- ❑ `Smarty/cache/`
- ❑ `Smarty/templates_c/`
- ❑ `modules/Emails/templates/`
- ❑ `modules/`
- ❑ `cron/modules/`
- ❑ `test/vtlib/`
- ❑ `backup/`
- ❑ `Smarty/templates/modules/`
- ❑ `test/wordtemplatedownload/`
- ❑ `test/product/`
- ❑ `test/user/`
- ❑ `test/contact/`
- ❑ `test/logo/`
- ❑ `logs/`
- ❑ `modules/Webmails/tmp/`

6.   Now, in a browser, navigate to the `index.php` file where you have extracted vtiger CRM to continue with Configuration Wizard.

To continue with the Configuration Wizard, skip to the section entitled *Using the Configuration Wizard*.

What just happened?

We just downloaded the vtiger CRM source code and installed it manually on a Windows computer or server that already has Apache web server, the PHP scripting language, and the MySQL database engine installed.

Installation on a Windows-based cloud server or dedicated server

If you want to install vtiger CRM on a Windows-based cloud server or dedicated server, the process is pretty much the same once you log in to your server instance and land on your Windows desktop.

Installation on Linux

There are many different versions of Linux, or distributions, as they are called. The most commonly used version of Linux today is Ubuntu, due to its large community and ease-of-use. We'll be using the latest **LTS (Long Term Support)** release, 10.04 called Lucid Lynx, because it includes PHP 5.3 and vtiger 5.2.1 now supports PHP 5.3. All of the instructions will be using the command line, so get your fingers ready.

You'll be able to use these exact same instructions on your desktop or on your cloud server.

System requirements

Let's briefly review the system requirements. These are found on the `vtiger.com` website:

- ◆ **Hardware minimum**: will run on a PC with at least x486 Pentium 4 with 256 MB RAM and 200 MB free disk space.
- ◆ **Hardware recommended**: x486 Pentium 4 with 512 MB RAM and 500 MB free disk space (I would recommend at least 1G).
- ◆ **Web browser**: Firefox 1.5.x and above. (Google Chrome also works nicely.)
- ◆ **Operating System**: Debian 4.0/5.0, Centos up-to 5.2, Fedora Core 6/9 (Ubuntu is a Debian-based system).

Installing vtiger CRM on Ubuntu Linux 10.04 LTS from source

The vtiger team has also created an installer for Linux to make our lives easier. However, there is still some configuration necessary. We'll cover all of those steps in the *Time for action section* below.

Time for action – installing vtiger on Linux (Ubuntu 10.04 LTS)

Let's install vtiger from source on our Ubuntu 10.04 LTS system. These instructions may also work on earlier versions of Ubuntu, but it's not guaranteed. It is easy to upgrade Ubuntu or to download the latest version and install it fresh.

To perform installation on Linux, specifically Ubuntu, it would be helpful to be familiar with the apt-get process of installing packages. But if you follow these tested steps very closely, then you should be able to install vtiger successfully.

Your Ubuntu computer will also have to be connected to the Internet, as the packages you'll be installing will be installed from Ubuntu servers over the Internet.

1. Open up a terminal or log into the cloud server via SSH:

```
ssh [USERNAME]@[SERVER_HOSTNAME]
```

For example:

```
ssh root@abcerver.com
```

2. Once you've logged in, let's make sure that the repositories are updated. The repositories are where Ubuntu gets its software from. Run the following in the terminal in order to edit the repositories using a text editor called `nano`. Since you're using `sudo`, you'll be asked for the root (or admin) password to run apt commands.

```
sudo nano /etc/apt/sources.list
```

3. Put the following two lines at the end of the file `/etc/apt/sources.list` and press *CTRL + O* to save it:

```
deb http://security.ubuntu.com/ubuntu maverick-security main
restricted multiverse

deb-src http://security.ubuntu.com/ubuntu maverick-security main
restricted multiverse
```

4. Now, press *CTRL-X* to exit the text editor.

5. Let's update the repositories. Execute the following command. You'll see all of the repositories updating.

```
sudo apt-get update
```

6. Now that the repositories are updated, let's install some packages. Run the following command in the terminal:

```
sudo apt-get install binutils cpp flex gcc libarchive-zip-perl
libc6-dev libcompress-zlib-perl libpcre3 libpopt-dev lynx m4
make  ncftp nmap openssl perl perl-modules unzip zip zlib1g-dev
autoconf automake1.9 libtool bison autotools-dev gcc libpng12-
dev libjpeg62-dev libfreetype6-dev libssl-dev libxml2-dev libxml2
apache2 php5-mysql libapache2-mod-php5 mysql-server php5-gd php5-
imap
```

7. When asked if you want to install the suggested packages, press *Y* and hit *Enter*. You'll see a lot of download and installing. When prompted, enter the password that you want to use for MySQL.

8. Once the packages have finished installing, change to the root directory of Apache:

```
cd /var/www
```

9. Download the source file (`vtigercrm-5.2.1.tar.gz`, or the latest version) that will install vtiger from the `vtiger.com` website:

```
http://downloads.sourceforge.net/project/vtigercrm/vtiger%20
CRM%205.2.1/Core%20Product/vtigercrm-5.2.1.tar.gz
```

10. Now unzip the tarball with the following command:

```
sudo tar -xvf vtigercrm-5.2.1.tar.gz
```

11. Before you begin the Configuration Wizard, however, we must make a few more changes. We need to modify the PHP settings. Execute the following command to open and edit the `php.ini` file:

```
sudo nano /etc/php5/apache2/php.ini
```

12. Find the following lines in the `php.ini` file and modify them to reflect the following. If any line is not present, add it into the file.

```
Zend.ze1_compatibility_mode = off
allow_call_time_reference = on
error_reporting = E_WARNING & E_NOTICE
safe_mode = off
display_errors = on
file_uploads = on
max_execution_time = 600
memory_limit = 32M
(You can set this higher if you see performance issues)
log_errors = off
output_buffering = on
register_globals = off
short_open_tag = On
```

13. Now that all of the PHP changes are complete, we have to restart the Apache web server for them to take effect. Execute the following code:

```
sudo /etc/init.d/apache2 restart
```

14. You may get a message about the server's domain name, but it should also display an [OK] message showing that it restarted successfully.

15. Now let's make the folders in the `vtigercrm` directory writable by the web server user:

```
sudo chown -R www-data: /var/www/vtigercrm
```

16. Now, you can navigate to the Configuration Wizard in your web browser. Go to:

❑ `http://[IP-ADDRESS]/vtigercrm/install.php` for a cloud server installation

❑ `http://localhost/vtigercrm/install.php` for a local installation

17. Now see the section entitled *Using the Configuration Wizard* to complete the installation on Ubuntu 10.04 LTS

What just happened?

On an Ubuntu Linux computer or server (version 10.04) we installed all of the software that vtiger depends on, including the Apache web server, the PHP scripting language, and the MySQL database engine. Then we downloaded the vtiger CRM source code and installed it manually. Now it's time for configuration.

Using the Configuration Wizard

Now that you've configured your web server successfully with vtiger extracted and ready to go, we have to go through the Configuration Wizard. This is the last step before we can log in and start using vtiger.

Time for action – configuring vtiger with the Configuration Wizard

1. In your browser, go to `http://localhost/vtigercrm` or `http://localhost:[port number]/vtigercrm` if you're using Apache on a port other than 80. Click **Install**:

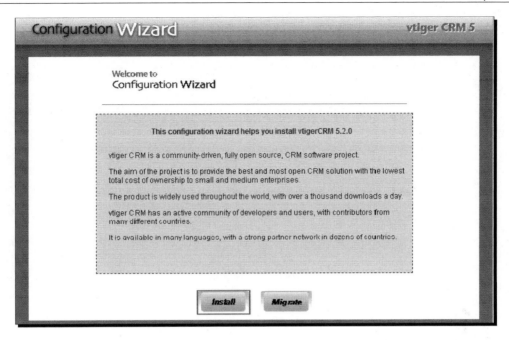

2. You may choose the read the license agreement. Click the **Next** button to accept the License agreement:

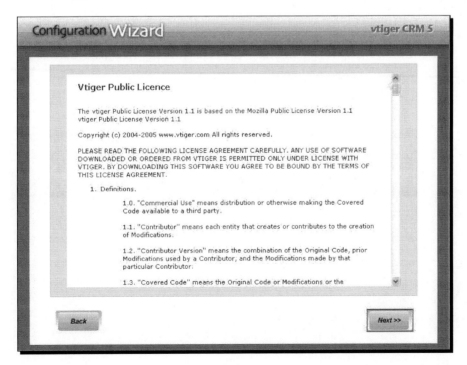

3. This page will check the `php.ini` values that you should have already configured in a previous step:

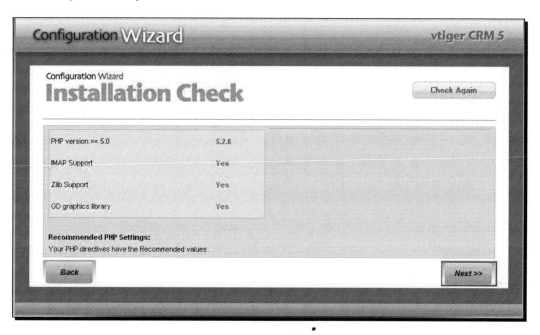

4. On this screen, you can enable additional modules to use in vtiger:

- ❑ The CustomerPortal allows your customers to receive a login to vtiger and participate in activities such as creating support tickets (trouble tickets), view quotes, and more.

- ❑ FieldFormulas allows you to auto fill values of different fields based on formulas and/or conditions.

- ❑ RecycleBin allows you to manage deleted records and restore them.

- ❑ Tooltip allows you to configure custom tooltip popups in the interface.

- ❑ Webforms allow you to create records, such as leads, in vtiger from your website or another web application.

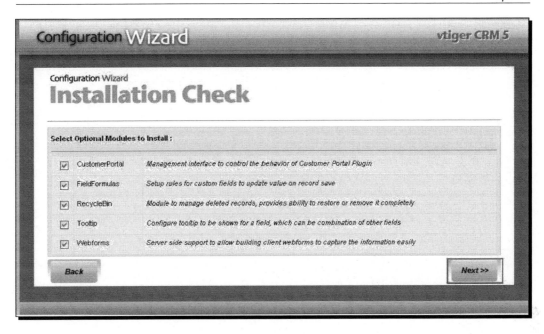

5. This page is for the database configuration:

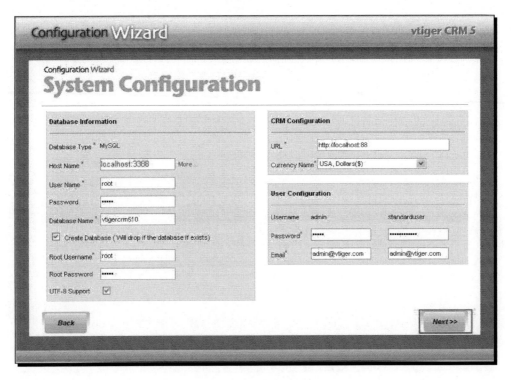

6. Let's first create the database. Go back to a terminal log into MySQL. If you haven't set a password for the root user, then use this command to log in:

```
mysql -u root
```

Otherwise:

```
mysql -u root -p [Your password]
```

7. Now, use the following command to create the vtiger CRM database:

```
mysql> CREATE DATABASE vtiger_db DEFAULT CHARACTER SET utf8
DEFAULT COLLATE utf8_general_ci;
```

8. Now create a vtiger user:

```
mysql> GRANT ALL ON vtiger_db.* TO 'vtigeruser'@'localhost'
IDENTIFIED BY 'SET_PASSWORD_HERE';
```

9. Now enter the root username and password you just chose into the MySQL configuration screen.

10. Also on this page make sure to enter the **email address** and **password** for the **admin** user.

11. Click on **Next** after you're entered all of the info:

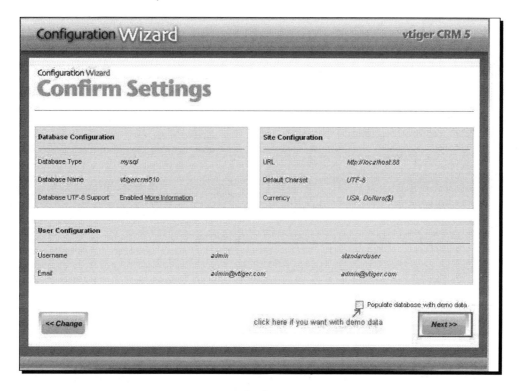

12. This page will show a confirmation of the database configuration made on the previous page. Check the **Populate Database With Demo Data** box if you want to install vtiger CRM with demo data or ignore it if you want to install with out demo data and click on the **Next** button. The demo data will allow you to see what vtiger CRM looks like with information in it. If you don't install the demo data, you will start with all empty screens. Installing the demo data may help you to get a feel of what vtiger can do for you.

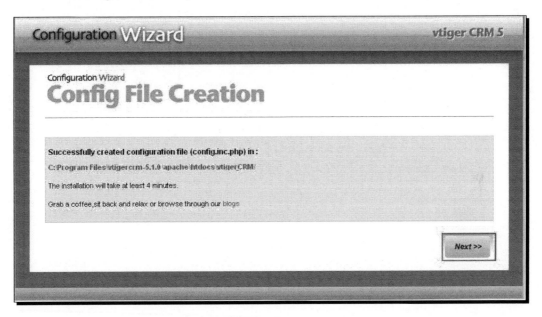

13. This page tells you where the configuration file (`config.inc.php`) is located and about how much time it will take to install.

14. Click on the **Next** button to finally install vtiger CRM:

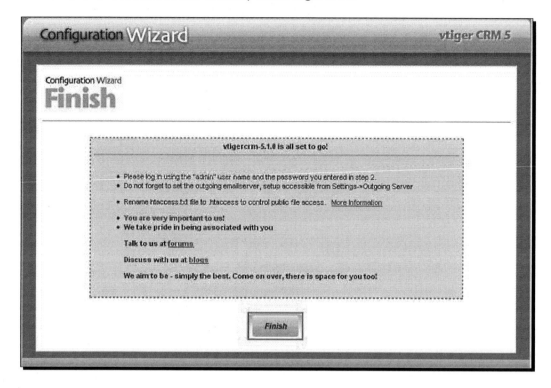

15. Click on the **Finish** button to complete the installation of vtiger CRM:

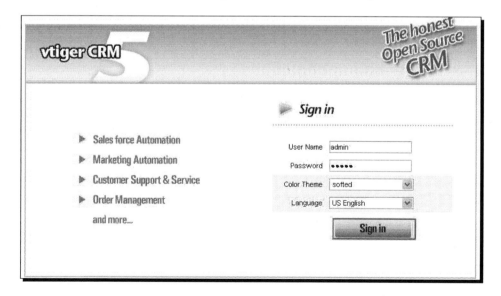

16. Clicking on **Finish** will take you to the login page where you can log in with the user name **admin** and the password you selected during the installation. You can change the password once you log in by clicking on the **Preferences** link at the top of the page.

What just happened?

You just successfully configured vtiger CRM! Congratulations!

Pop quiz – Installing vtiger CRM

1. What's the difference between installing with an installer and installing from source?

    a. A technician comes to my house and I don't have to do anything.

    b. The installer uses an easy, "wizard" approach whereas installing from source requires more time and knowledge.

    c. The source code isn't installed when you use the installer.

2. What are the different packages that you have installed as prerequisites in Ubuntu 10.04 LTS? (Have fun with that one.)

    a. Apache Web Server, PHP and MySQL, and other needed software.

    b. The ones that came in the mail from UPS.

    c. What packages?

3. What is the Configuration Wizard? Does it handle the entire vtiger CRM installation process?

    a. Yes, the wizard takes care of the entire installation.

    b. It installs vtiger using magic.

    c. The configuration wizard only configures vtiger after the source code is installed.

Summary

We learned a lot in this chapter regarding vtiger CRM installation.

Specifically, we covered:

◆ Installing vtiger CRM on Windows using the installer:

We learned how to take the quick route and use a nice little installer package created by the vtiger team to install vtiger on a Windows 2000, XP, Vista, or Windows 7 system.

◆ Installing vtiger CRM on Windows from source:

We learned how to download and install the vtiger source code on a web server system that is already configured with Apache, PHP, and MySQL.

◆ Installing vtiger CRM on Linux from source:

We learned how to install and configure vtiger on an Ubuntu Linux 10.04 LTS system by installing the necessary Apache, PHP, and MySQL packages and then installing the vtiger source code.

Now that we've learned how to install vtiger, we're ready to sink our claws into it. Let's start entering data and playing around. In the next chapter, we'll log into vtiger and start using it.

3

And the Claws Come Out—Getting Started with vtiger

So, we have vtiger installed. Now what? Now we can start entering company-related data like our contacts, our leads, our accounts—all that good stuff.

In this chapter we shall:

◆ Enter company data

◆ Import CRM entities like leads and accounts

◆ Create users and set permissions

◆ Configure email

◆ Configure backup

So let's get on with it...

Entering company data

The first thing we should do is enter our company data. This data will be used on system correspondence like emails and PDF documents such as invoices.

Time for action – entering company data

To enter company data, do the following:

1. Go to **Settings**:

2. Click on **Company Details**:

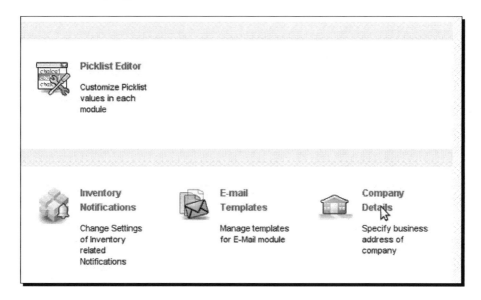

3. Now, on the **Company Details** screen, click on the **Edit** button and edit the information:

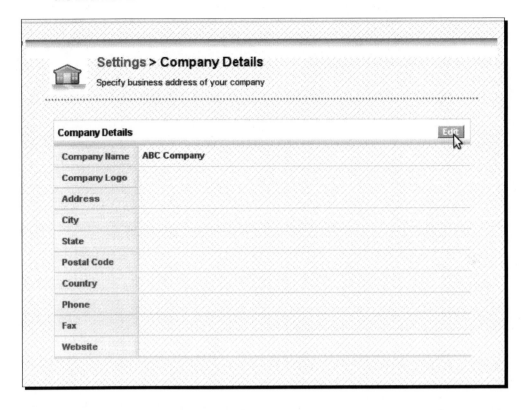

4. Now, enter all of your company information and browse for your company logo:

 Make sure that it is in true JPG format, because that is required for its use in PDF files. If you use a GIF or PNG format image and just change the extension to .jpg, it won't work in the PDF files.

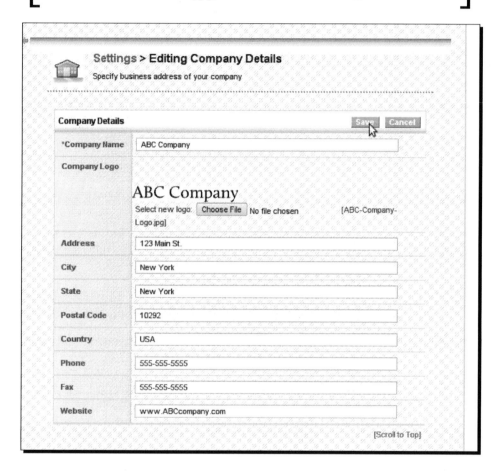

5. Now click **Save**.

Now your company info has been entered and your logo has been uploaded.

What just happened?

We just entered our company information into vtiger. Now it will be used in template emails and PDF documents such as invoices and purchase orders.

Now we're ready to start importing customer data.

Importing customer data

Let's import some leads. This process is the same for importing leads, accounts, contacts, and potentials. You can only import a `.csv` file (comma separated values) to make sure that, you save the excel file in CSV format before trying to import it. It also helps to have meaningful headers in your data. This will make the data mapping process easier.

Time for action – importing customer data

We're going to import leads in this example, but you can use this same process to import accounts, contacts, and potentials.

 NOTE: You should import only a few records before importing everything just to make sure you've mapped everything properly. Also, use a CSV format that wraps all of the values in commas so they can contain commas.

1. Prepare your CSV file. Make it neat with meaningful headers:

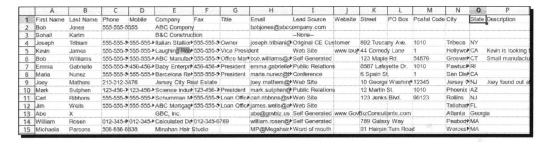

2. Go to **Sales | Leads**:

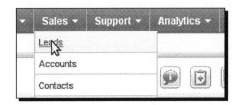

3. Click on the **Import** icon:

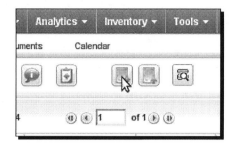

4. On this next screen, Browse for the `.csv` file that you want to upload and click on **Next**:

5. If you'll be making an import with a file just like this many times in the future, then check the box **Save as Custom Mapping** and give it a name. The next time it will appear in the dropdown above labeled as **Use Saved Mapping**.

6. You'll be shown a list of your header names and then a series of drop down lists with vtiger's field names. Now map each one to your columns in the CSV file. Then click on **Import Now**. (You can opt to do Duplicate Merging if you want to, but we're not going to cover it in this section.)

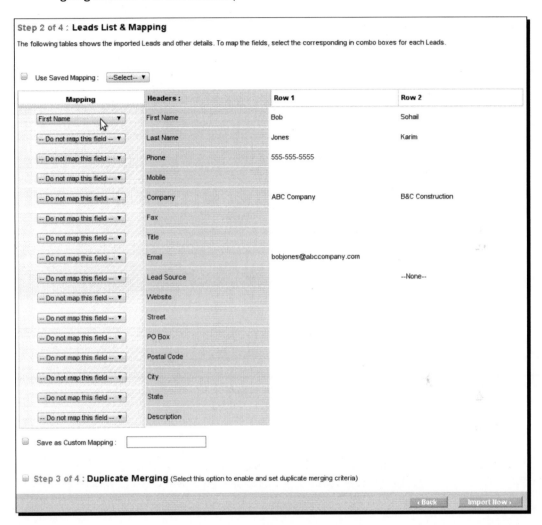

7. You'll be shown a success message and a list of the last several leads that were imported. Click on **Finished** to return to the default list of view of your newly imported leads:

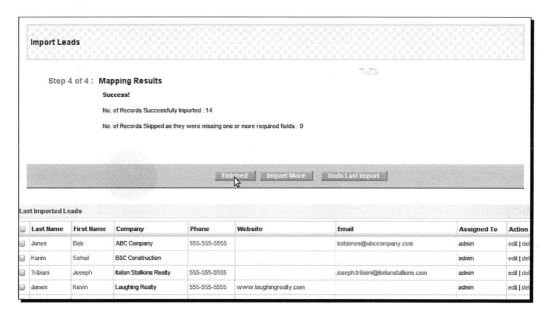

What just happened?

We just imported some leads into vtiger. You can use the same exact process to import account, contacts, and potentials. They will each have their unique set of fields to deal with.

Note that we have some basic data in vtiger, we can invite our team to start using vtiger.

Creating users

A very sophisticated and granular, role-based security model is available in vtiger. You can control a user's access to specific modules—you can even restrict access to specific fields. You can also control users' access to each other's data.

We're going to go create some users together and then we're going to assign them some specific permissions so we can get an idea of how we can use this elegant model. It has the potential to be highly complex. We're not going to go really in-depth here, but we're going to get a comprehensive overview of the model so we can feel empowered to mirror our organization's structure within vtiger. If you are a small organization with only a few users that have access to all of the data, then you can most likely skip this section and just create your users with full access.

If you are going to create complex permission structure, you first need to create any custom fields in vtiger so that they can be included in that structure.

An overview of the user model

Let's briefly consider the user model in vtiger. The user model consists of profiles, roles, and users. Users can also be arranged in groups. So, how does it all work together?

Profiles

A profile in vtiger represents a set of actions that a user can perform, such as using certain modules and viewing/editing certain records. Access to specific fields and import/export tools is also managed in profiles. Global or default privileges are also set for a profile. The profile can start off with **View All** or **Edit All** privileges or it can be set to **View None** or **Edit None** by default, and thereby, only explicit privileges would be granted. The screenshot gives you an idea of how a profile works.

By default, there are four profiles in vtiger: Administrator, Sales, Support, and Guest. They all have certain access privileges. Then each of the profiles is assigned to a role.

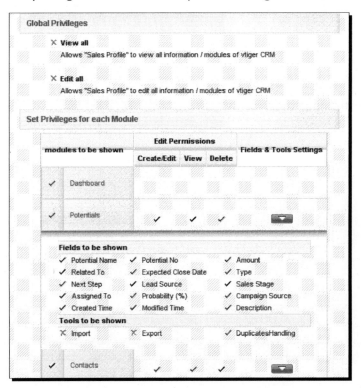

Roles

Roles can be likened to a position in a company like Sales Manager. It can be used for several people that all have the same function and, therefore, privileges to access important company information. Each role also specifies who they report to, creating a hierarchy:

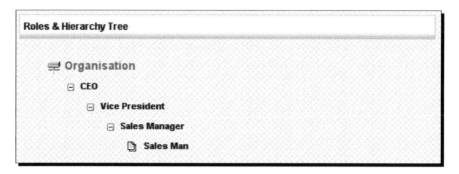

Roles can also be assigned several different **Profiles**. This could come in handy if someone wears two different hats. For instance, Joe is the **Sales Manager**, but he also participates in support operations. So, you could create a role called Sales and Support Manager and assign the **Support Profile** to his role as well:

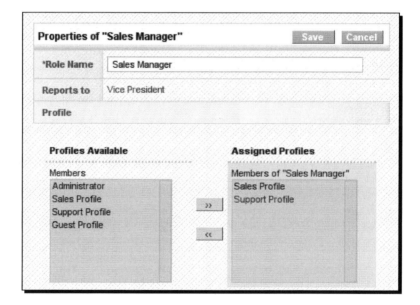

Users

Finally, we come to users. In vtiger, you're either a standard user or you're an administrator. There are the two types of users. Basically, a standard user's access is limited while an administrator's is not. An administrator has full access to everything.

Setting up our team in vtiger

Let's assume that we'll have the following people on our team:

◆ **Brad Armstrong, CEO**: Brad will have access to all modules and all data within the system. Setting up his permissions should be easy.

◆ **Jack Thurgood, Sales Manager**: Jack reports to Brad and will have access to sales-related modules, such as contacts, leads, accounts, opportunities, and products. He will also have access to the calendar and email modules. He will have to create/edit, view, and delete permissions for these modules. He will be able to view all records for those users that work below him in the organization.

◆ **Tom Sherman, Sales Representative**: Tom reports to Jack and will have access to all sales-related modules, such as contacts, leads, accounts, and opportunities. He will also have access to the calendar and email modules. He will have create/edit and view permissions for these modules but he will not be able to delete records. He will only be able to view records that are assigned to him.

◆ **Lars Haskins, Support**: Lars will be supporting customer issues. He'll have access to the accounts module, the trouble ticket module, and the products module. He will have to create/edit, view, and delete permissions for the trouble ticket module and he will only have view permissions for the accounts and products modules. He will be able to view all records within these modules.

Now let's set up the profiles, roles, and users for our team.

Time for action – setting up user permissions for the CEO

1. Set up Brad's profile by going to **Settings | Profiles**:

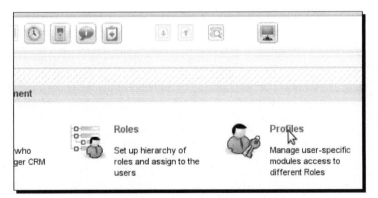

2.   Then click the **New Profile** button:

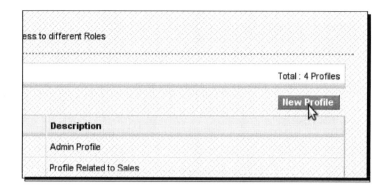

3.   Give the profile a name and a description and choose **Administrator** as the base profile and click on **Next**:

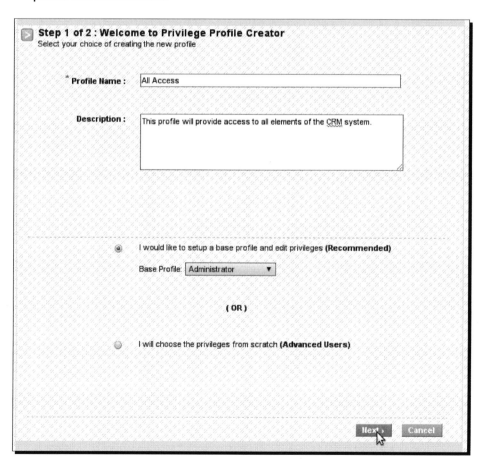

4. Now check the boxes labeled **View All** and **Edit All** and click on **Finish**:

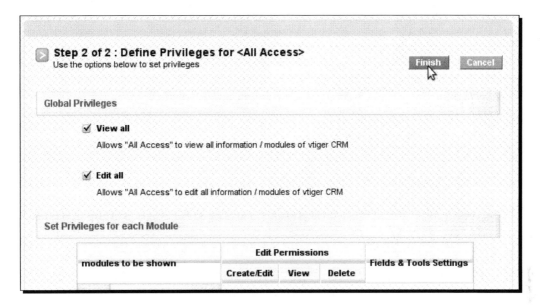

5. You can now see your newly created profile:

6. Now let's set up the role for the Brad as CEO. Go to **Settings | Roles**:

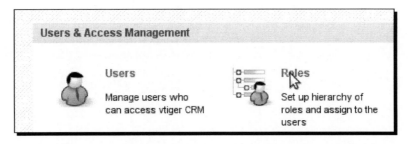

7. Now, to add a new role, hover over the word **Organization** in the hierarchy tree and click on the little plus sign that pops up:

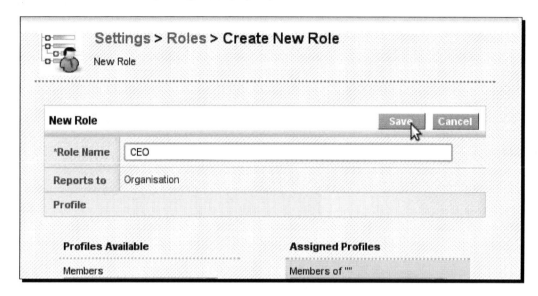

8. Give the role a name, add the **All Access** profile, and click on **Save**:

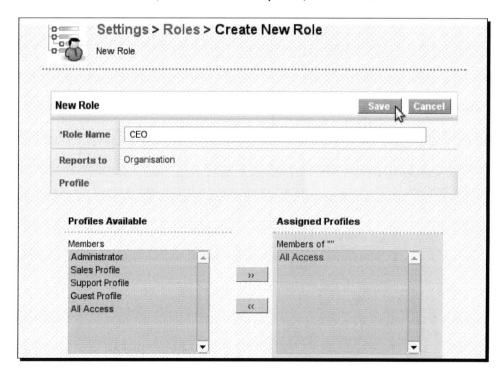

9. Now you can see your newly created role, CEO, at the top of the hierarchy right under organization:

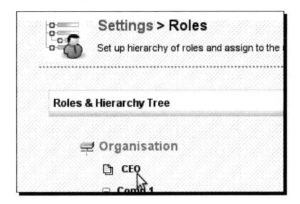

10. Now that we've setup the profile and the role, we can now set up a user account for Brad. Go to **Settings | Users**:

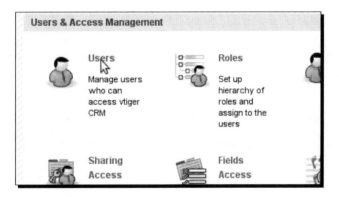

11. Click on the **New User** button:

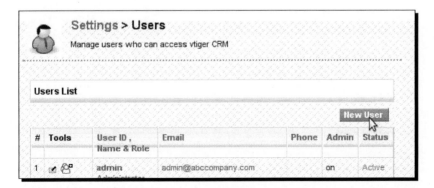

12. Enter all of the required information in Section 1 and choose the **CEO** role that we created for Brad's role. Sections 2 through 8 are optional. Click on **Save**:

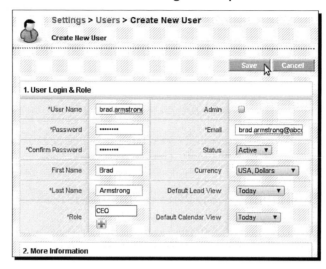

13. Now Brad will receive an email with his user account information. You can see that all modules come up in the menu. He can also view all records including those that are not assigned to him. He does not have access to the **Settings** section as he is not an administrator:

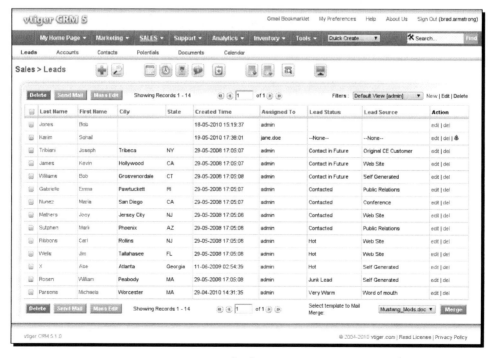

What just happened?

We just set up the fictional CEO, Brad, with full access to all parts of vtiger CRM. We did this by creating a **role**, **profile**, and a **user** account for him.

Now's let's set up our sales manager, Jack Thurgood.

Time for action – setting up user permissions for the sales manager

1. Let's set up the Sales Manager profile for Jack Thurgood. Go to **Settings | Profiles**:

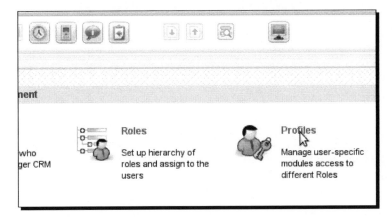

2. Click the **New Profile** button:

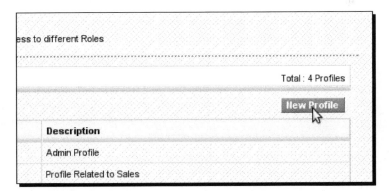

3. Give the profile a name and a description and click **Next**:

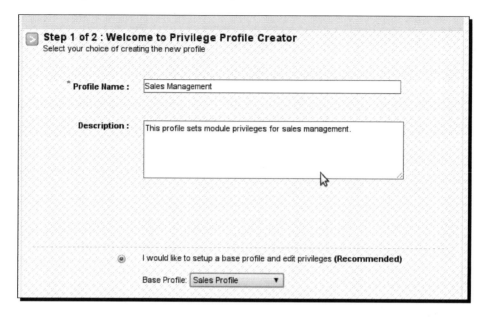

4. On the next page check off **View All** and **Edit All** since Jack will have these privileges. Then for the modules—according to the privileges we established in the section *Setting Up Our Team in vtiger*, check the boxes for **Potentials**, **Contacts**, **Accounts**, **Leads**, **Calendar**, **Email**, and **Products**. For the sake of this example, we'll uncheck the rest of the modules. Then click on **Finish**.

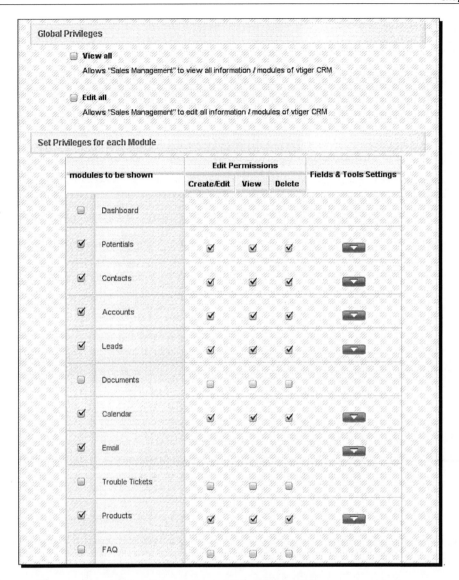

5. Now let's set up a **Role** for Jack. Go to **Settings | Roles**:

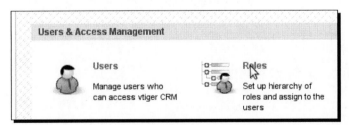

6. Since we want Jack to report to Brad, the CEO, let's hover the mouse over **CEO** and click the **plus sign** that pops up to create a role that reports to Brad:

7. Now call this **Role Sales Manager** and add the **Sales Management** profile. Then click on **Save**:

8. Now you can see the **Sales Manager** role you've just created in the hierarchy tree:

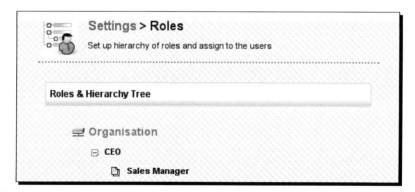

9. Finally, let's create a user account for Jack. Go **Settings | Users**:

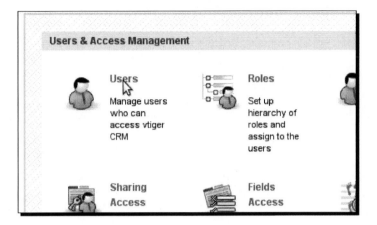

10. Click on the **New User** button:

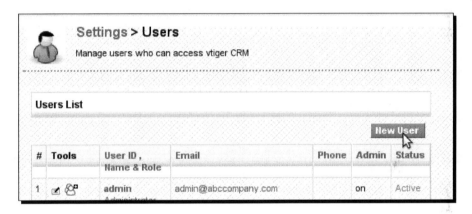

11. Now fill out all of the information in, at least, section 1 and make sure to choose the **Sales Manager** role for Jack. Then click on **Save**:

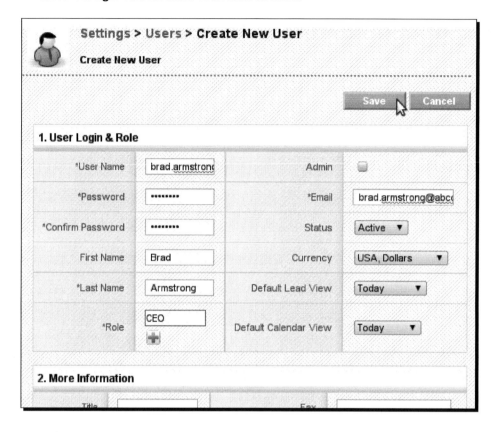

12. Now, notice that when Jack logs in, he can't see all of the modules, but only the ones that have been enabled for him:

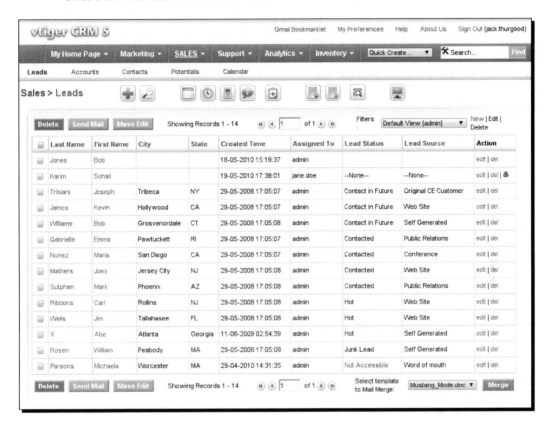

What just happened?

We just set up the fictional sales manager, Jack Thurgood, with full access to a subset of data and modules related to sales operations in vtiger CRM. We did this by creating a role, profile, and a user account for him. Now, let's set up our sales rep, Tom Sherman.

Time for action – setting up user permissions for a sales representative

1. Let's first set up a profile for a sales rep. Go to **Settings | Profiles**:

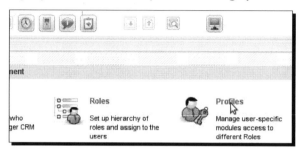

2. Then click on the **New Profile** button:

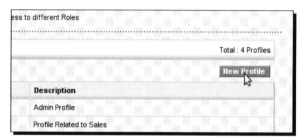

3. Let's create a profile called **Front End Sales** and give it a description. Choose **Sales Profile** as a base profile. Click on **Next**:

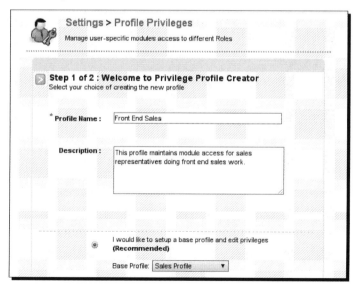

4. Since Tom will be more restricted than those above him, there are a few more changes to make on the next screen. First uncheck **View All** and **Edit All**. But make the changes according to the privileges we established in *Setting Up Our Team in vtiger* section. Tom won't be able to delete anything. You can go a step further to restrict the fields he can see by clicking the down arrow in the **Fields & Tool Settings** column. Click on **Finish** when you're done:

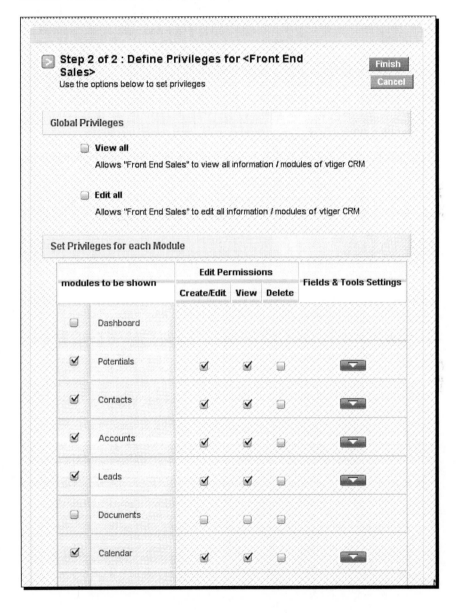

5. Now let's create the sales representative role. Go to **Settings | Roles**:

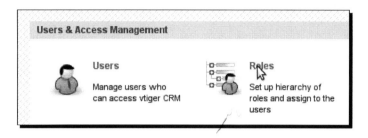

6. Now, hover over the **Sales Manager** role and click the plus sign that pops up to create role that reports to a Sales Manager:

7. Let's call the role **Sales Representative** and add the **Front End Sales** profile we just created:

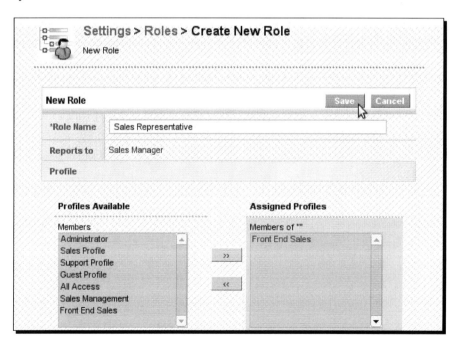

8. Now, because we want Tom to only be able to view records that are assigned to him, we have to go into **Settings | Sharing Access**:

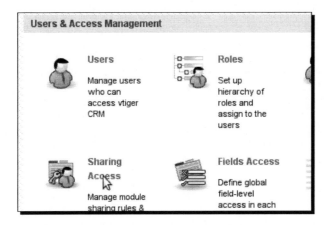

9. Since we only want Tom to be able to view Contacts, Accounts, Potentials, and Leads that are assigned to him, let's click on the **Change Privileges** button:

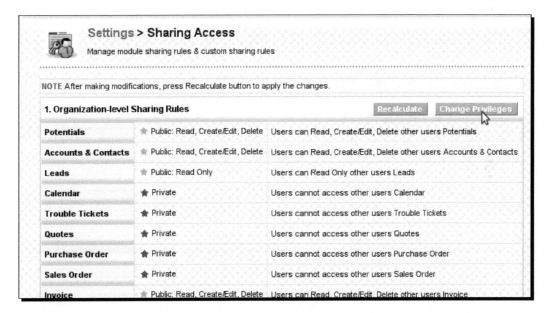

10. From the dropdown box, choose **Private** for each of the modules **Potentials, Accounts & Contacts**, and **Leads**. You should receive a message when you change Accounts & Contacts to Private saying that you must set other modules to Private as well. Click on **Save Permissions**:

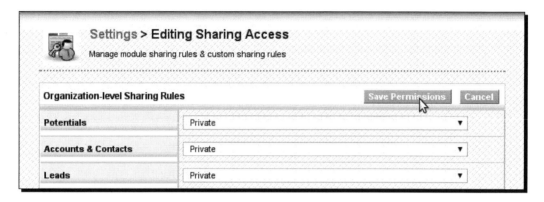

11. Now recalculate the privileges on all records by clicking on **Recalculate**:

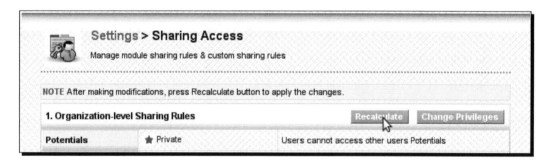

12. Now we must allow access to the CEO and Sales Management to see the records assigned to Sales Representatives. Scroll down on the same screen to **2. Custom Sharing Rules**. Click on **Add Privileges**:

13. On the popup screen, choose **Roles::Sales Representative** for Step 1 and then **Roles::Sales Manager** for Step 2. Choose **Read/Write** under **Permissions**. Click on **Add Rule**:

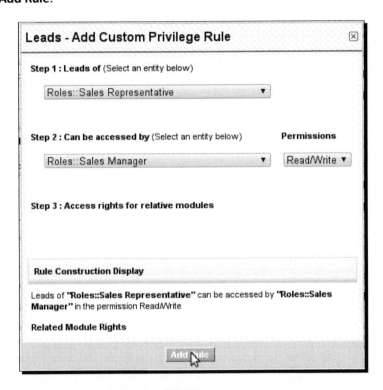

14. Repeat steps 12 and 13 for **Accounts & Contacts** and **Potentials**.

15. Finally, **Recalculate** privileges once again.

16. We still have yet to create a user account for Tom. Let's go to **Settings | Users**:

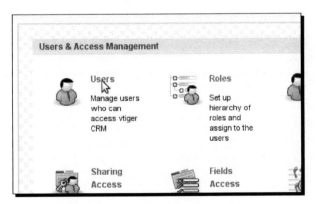

17. Click **New User**:

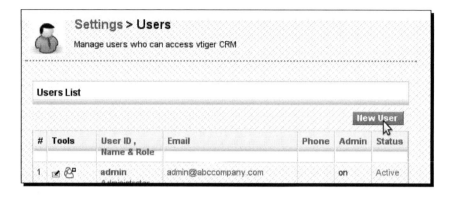

18. Again, enter all of the info into section 1 and choose the **Sales Representative** role we created. Then click on **Save**:

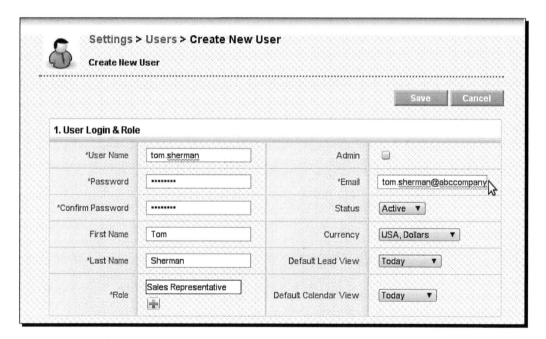

19. Now, when we login as Tom, we can see that he can see only records assigned to him and everyone above him in the organization can also see what is assigned to him. He can only see a limited number of modules. He can't see any leads because he hasn't created any. There are leads in the system, but he can't see them:

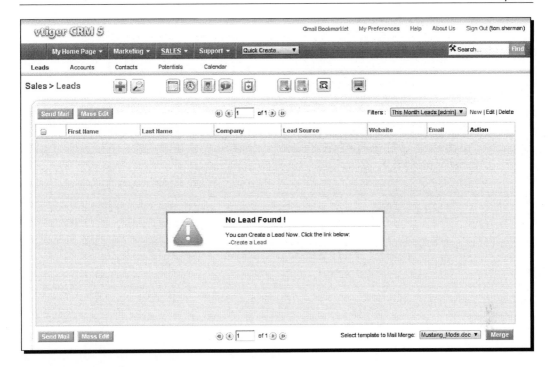

What just happened?

We just set up the fictional sales representative, Tom Sherman, with partial access to sales-related data and modules in vtiger CRM. We did this by creating a role, profile, and a user account for him. Tom does not have access to other sales representative's data.

Now we can create our support guy, Lars.

Time for action – setting up user permissions for our support guy

1. Let's first set up a profile for a support person. Go to **Settings | Profiles**:

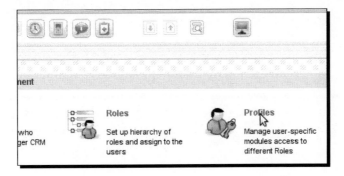

2. Then click the **New Profile** button:

3. Let's call this profile **Support** and give it a description. Let's choose **Administrator** as the base profile. Click on **Next**:

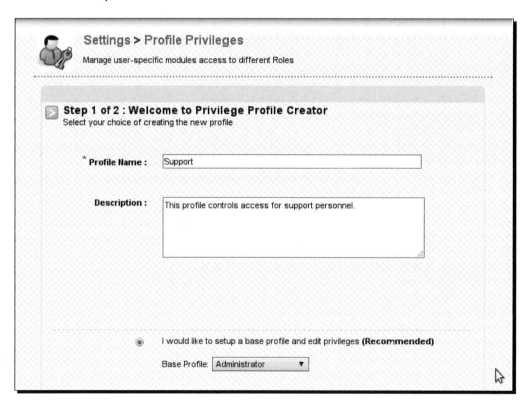

4. Lars will have very limited access according to the privileges we established in the section *Setting up our team in vtiger*. Click on **Finish**:

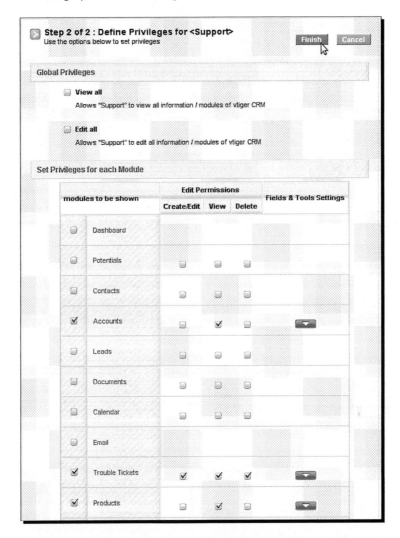

5. Now, let's create a role for Lars. Go to **Settings | Roles**:

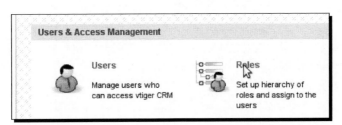

6. Hover over the **CEO** role and click on the plus sign that pops up:

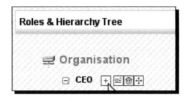

7. Let's call the role **Support Representative** and assign the **Support** profile to it. Click on **Save**:

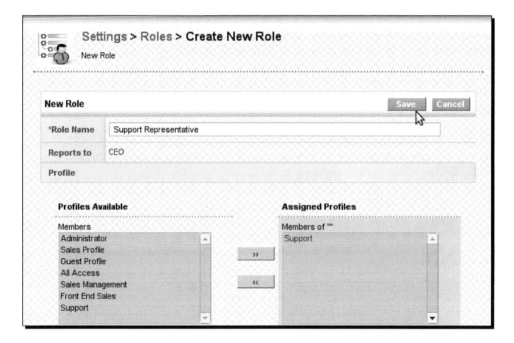

8. Now we can see the new **Support Representative** role we've created in the hierarchy tree:

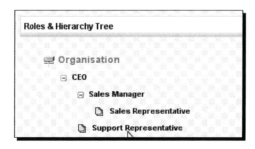

9. Finally let's create a user account for Lars by going to **Settings | Users**:

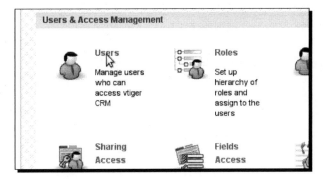

10. Click on the **New User** button:

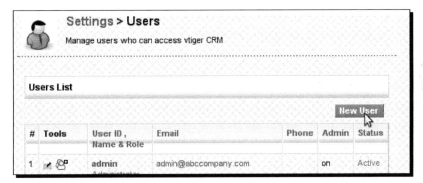

11. Now enter all of the information into Section 1 and choose the **Support Representative** role. Click on **Save**:

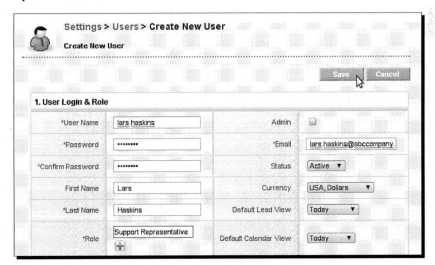

12. Now when we log in as Lars Haskins, notice that he can't even create an account. He has very limited access:

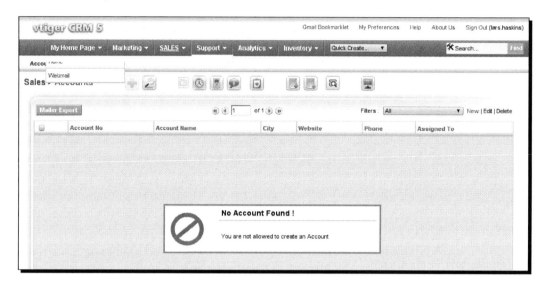

He can create and manage trouble tickets though.

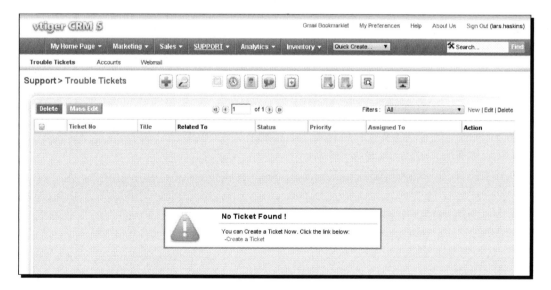

What just happened?

We just set up the fictional support representative, Lars, with access to support-related data and modules in vtiger CRM. We did this by creating a role, profile, and a user account for him. Lars does not have access to data that he does not need to see.

Now our team is ready to start using the system—creating leads, contacts and accounts, and servicing customers through the support system.

Have a go hero

Now that you've been able to create a few different roles, profiles, and user accounts for different scenarios, try out some of your own scenarios, perhaps from within your own company. You could try to create a user that has view-only access to everything, perhaps for an investor. Or perhaps you have a partner company that sends you leads and you want them to have view/create/edit access to leads. Give it a shot.

Pop quiz

1. What is a Profile in vtiger CRM?

   a. A page displaying background information about a user

   b. A user photo shot from the side

   c. A set of access privileges that will allow certain actions

2. What is a Role in vtiger CRM?

   a. A part in the company's annual Broadway play

   b. A hierarchical position that determines a user's function in the company

   c. vtiger's way of tracking employee attendance

3. What does a user account consist of in vtiger CRM?

   a. A username and password to log in to vtiger

   b. Information that identifies the user

   c. Administrator access or standard access

   d. All of the above

Configuring e-mail

vtiger sends email messages automatically from time to time, such as calendar event notifications, messages generated by workflow, and so on. In order for this to work properly, we'll need to set up the Outgoing Server settings in the Settings section.

Time for action – setting up outgoing e-mail

1. Go to **Settings | Outgoing Server**:

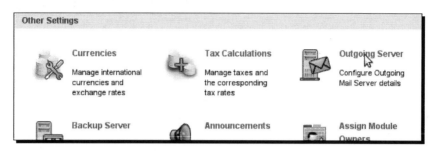

2. If you're doing it for the first time, you may not have to click on **Edit** on the next screen. Otherwise, click the **Edit** button:

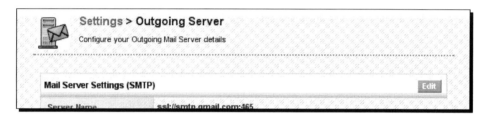

3. Since Gmail is a popular email service, we'll show you how to use Gmail for outgoing email. Fill out the fields using the following format for Gmail. Otherwise, you may not have to specify the port number. Click on **Save**:

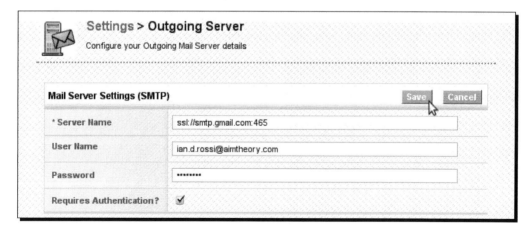

Now you're ready to send outgoing messages from vtiger!

What just happened?

We successfully configured outgoing email to work with Gmail's SMTP server.

Now, let's set up the Webmail client so that we can check out incoming email from within vtiger.

Time for action – setting up the mail client

1. Go to **My Home Page| Webmail**:

2. If it's your first time, you'll see a link **Incoming MailServer Settings**. Click on it. If it's not your first time logging in, your screen will look like the following:

3. Before filling out the information on the next screen, you'll have to get the IMAP server information from your email service provider or from your in-house IT manager or system administrator. Fill out all of the information required, such as the server name/IP address and **SSL** options. Click on **Save**:

4. It may take a few minutes, but vtiger will load all of the mail in your Inbox. You should also be able to see any folders in your IMAP account.

vtiger has an issue as of version 5.1 with the Webmail client. If you don't keep your inbox very light, as in under 10 messages, the client can start to act very slow. It can actually slow down the rest of the entire system. This is something that the vtiger team is working on rectifying in future versions. Using the webclient is not mandatory. I recommend using either the Outlook or Thunderbird plugins as an alternative.

What just happened?

We just entered our IMAP email server information into vtiger. Specifically, we entered the email server information from our Gmail account. We can now view the email in our inbox without leaving vtiger. We can simply go to **My Home Page | Webmail**.

Configuring vtiger backup

Now that we have everything set up, we want to make sure that we protect all of the time we just invested into vtiger. Let's use the backup feature of vtiger to secure our data and the processes that we've set in place in vtiger.

Time for action – setting up vtiger backups

1. Go to **Settings | Backup Server**:

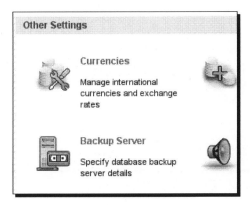

2. Let's set up local backup first. Create a folder on the computer vtiger is hosted on; you'll use this for backup. On my Ubuntu Linux computer, I'm creating the folder `/var/www/vtigercrm/backup`. On Windows you could make a folder like `C:\vtiger\backup`.

3. Now, on the **Backup Server** screen, enter that location into the **Backup Location** field:

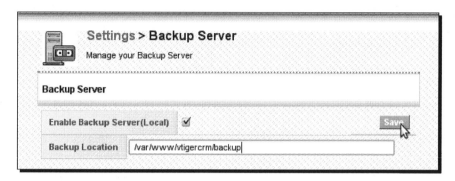

4. Now let's set up a backup to an FTP server. This way, you can have an onsite and an offsite backup. First, you'll need to get the FTP server details from your FTP hosting provider or your IT person or system administrator.

5. Now, enter it into bottom half of the **Backup Server** page, under **Server Address, User Name**, and **Password**. Then click on **Save**. I'm using the hosted FTP space on `aimtheoryCRM.com` that I set up for this book.

Make sure you enter the FTP server address without the `ftp://` prefix.

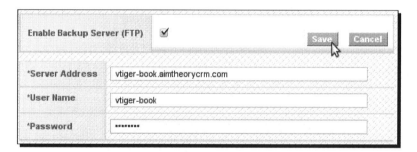

Now vtiger is ready to backup onsite and offsite!

NOTE: This process only backs up the database. Your configuration files and stored documents will not be backed up by this process. Your system administrator should also set up a scheduled backup of vtiger CRM's entire file system.

What just happened?

Backup has now been set up. vtiger will back up your CRM data to a folder on the local hosted computer. It will also back up data to a remote FTP server to protect against a physical disaster where vtiger is being hosted.

Summary

We learned a lot in this chapter about getting started with vtiger.

Specifically, we covered:

◆ Entering company data

◆ Importing data

◆ Creating users and system access

◆ Configuring email

◆ Configuring regular system backup

Now that we've covered the basics about getting started with vtiger, we're ready to dig in and start using it in our day-to-day business. Let's move on to Chapter 4 where we'll investigate this in more detail.

4
Leashing the Beast—Using vtiger

There's plenty of information on the Internet and on the vtiger forums related to how to install, configure, and customize vtiger. However, simple day-to-day usage is not covered well. In this chapter, we will learn how to use vtiger in day-to-day operations. Many CRM implementations fail, including vtiger implementations, because of lack of training and, therefore, understanding of how to go about using vtiger to manage sales processes and other business critical processes.

In this chapter, we'll discuss the following:

◆ How to use vtiger's interface to your advantage:
   ❑ Home page dashboard
   ❑ Quick create
   ❑ Shortcuts
   ❑ Using vtiger's main detail view
   ❑ Using actions
◆ Managing lists
   ❑ Assigning leads and accounts to users
   ❑ Using filters
◆ Cross-linking CRM data
◆ Storing documents
◆ Tracking customer communication via email

By the end of this chapter, you will have overcome any perception of mystery regarding vtiger and will feel confident and eager to start using vtiger in your own day-to-day routine.

So let's get on with it...

How to use vtiger's interface to your advantage

While vtiger's interface is admittedly not perfect—or ideal for some—it is one of the reasons that many organizations choose it over other open source CRM tools, like SugarCRM. vtiger CRM's interface is more intuitive and is actually quicker.

In this section we'll take you on a brief tour of the interface and how you can use it to get things done efficiently.

Home page dashboard

The home page dashboard is designed to give you an overview, at a glance, of important CRM-related information such as meetings, to-dos, and key performance indicators (KPIs):

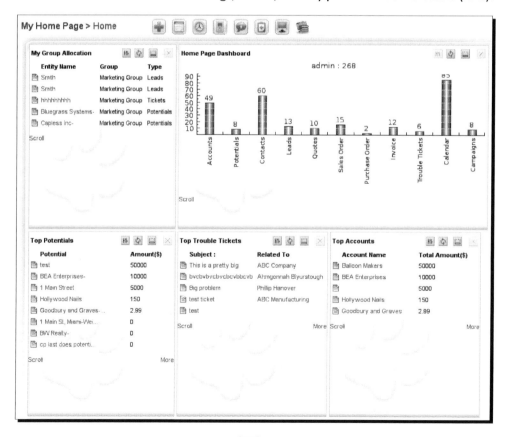

If you're a sales professional, for example, you can see the top potential sales you have in your pipeline and also see any new leads you've entered into the system or that have been assigned to you.

If you're in a support role, you can see what trouble tickets have been assigned to you.

If you're a sales manager, you can see how many leads, potentials, and accounts are in the system and if your sales team is making progress.

Since the dashboard is interactive, you can click your way to a lead or account that you're interested in and you'll be sent straight to the detail.

Let's configure the dashboard for our needs.

Time for action – how to configure the home page dashboard

1. Just click on the **My Preferences** link in the header:

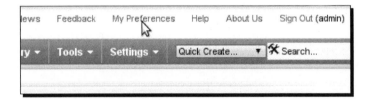

2. Now click on the **Edit** button:

3. Now just scroll down to the bottom, to section **7. Home Page Components** and choose to show or hide each component in the dashboard according to your own needs. Then click on **Save**:

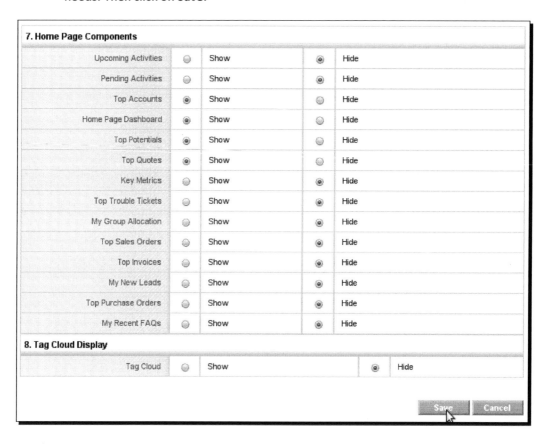

4. You will now be sent back to the **My Preferences** page and you can see your saved changes.

5. Now, click on the **My Home Page** to return to your dashboard:

6. Now we can see only the dashboard components that we've selected to show by clicking the **Show** radio button. The others are hidden.

NOTE: If you've selected to show Upcoming Activities or Pending Activities, but there are none in the system, then those panels will show up in the dashboard, but they will contain a message indicating that there is no data present.

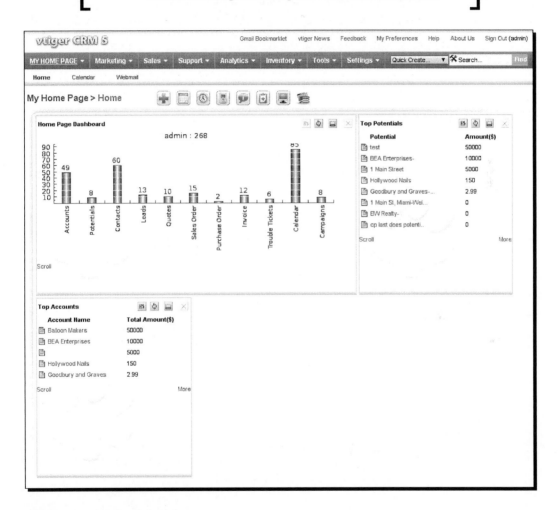

What just happened?

We have successfully modified our home page dashboard to show only the components that are applicable to us.

How to use Quick Create

The Quick Create feature is designed to save time in getting data into the system. With Quick Create, you can enter leads, accounts, and other information without having to go through multiple clicks and waiting for page loads.

Let's try it.

Time for action – using Quick Create

1. Click on the **Quick Create** menu to the right of the main module menu and then choose **New Lead**:

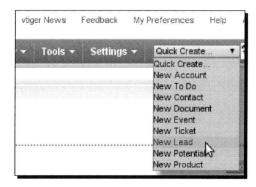

2. Now, you'll see a form pop up without any page reload. Fill it in and click on **Save**:

3. Now our lead is in the system:

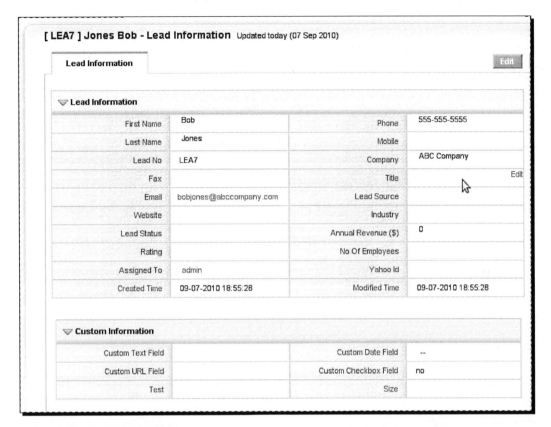

What just happened?

We used the **Quick Create** feature to create a lead easily with only one page load. You use the Quick Create feature to create accounts, to-dos, contacts, potentials, tickets, and more.

Using the shortcut icons

The shortcut icons that appear just underneath the main menu provide quick access to common tasks and tools. Different icons appear in this area depending on what you're doing in vtiger.

On the Home Page, you'll see the following items:

◆ The first icon, the **plus sign**, will allow you to **Create** or **Add** new CRM records. For instance, if you are working in the **Leads** module, clicking on the plus sign will allow you to create a new lead:

◆ Following the Add function, you'll also have access to your **calendar**. Clicking on the calendar icon will open up a 30 day calendar view without refreshing the page:

◆ Next we have a **clock** icon. Naturally, clicking this icon will open a clock. Except it is a world clock and you'll have an option to switch between time zones:

◆ Next we have a **calculator** icon. Clicking this will open a calculator:

◆ The **little bubble** icon allows you to **chat** with other users that are online:

◆ The **little clipboard** with the green back arrow is the **Last Viewed** menu, which allows you to see information in the system that you've looked at recently:

Now click on **Sales | Leads**. You'll notice there are a few more icons that show up when you're in a list view of leads, accounts, and so on. Here is what they look like:

◆ Notice the two **hard drive icons** with the respective down and up green arrows. These are the **import** and **export** icons. They allow you to import and export CRM records, which we have discussed in Chapter 3:

◆ The little magnifying glass icon to the right of the import/export icons allow you to **search for duplicates**:

◆ The **little computer screen** icon is the **View All** function, which gives you quick access to every feature of the system:

◆ Finally, the last hammer icon on the right takes you to the **Settings** page for the module you're working in. There you can view and change layout elements using the **Layout Editor**, which we'll discuss in Chapter 5, the next chapter:

Using vtiger's main detail view

Before we take at look at the detail view, let's enable vtiger's single pane view. This will allow us to look at all related information in one place rather than having an **Other Information** tab.

Just go to **Settings | Default Module View** and make sure that the **Enable Singlepane View** box is checked. vtiger's main detail view is where a sales professional will spend a good deal of time, since it will provide all of the vital information about your customers, or those soon-to-be:

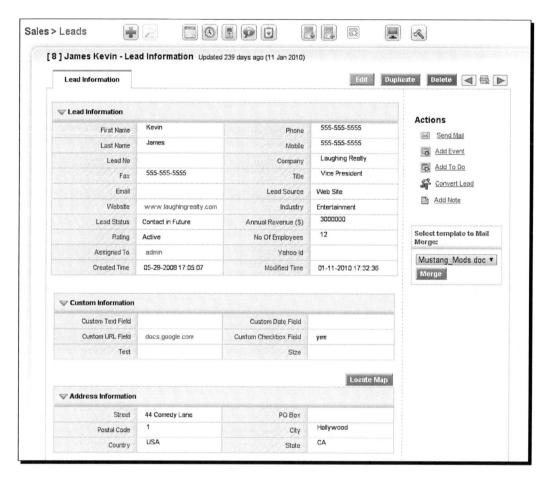

The main detail view allows you to get a single view of your customer. It's possible to see, not only contact information, but emails that you've sent to the customer, their sales process history, any products associated with them, and much more:

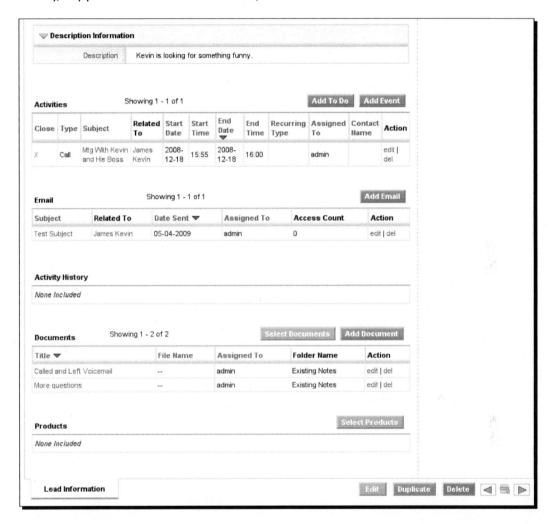

Using actions

On the details screen of any CRM record—leads, accounts, and so on—you'll see a list of **Actions** to the right side of the screen:

Using the Actions menu, you can:

◆ **Send an email**

◆ **Add an event related to the person/company**

◆ **Add a to-do**

◆ **Convert a lead**

◆ **Add notes**

These can save you lots of time, since you don't have to click into the Calendar section and then manually add the event and choose to relate it to a customer or lead.

Time for action – using actions to convert a lead

Let's try out one of the actions and convert this lead, Kevin James, to an account. By converting the Lead, Kevin will also become a contact that is related to the account under his company name.

1. From the lead detail screen, click Convert Lead:

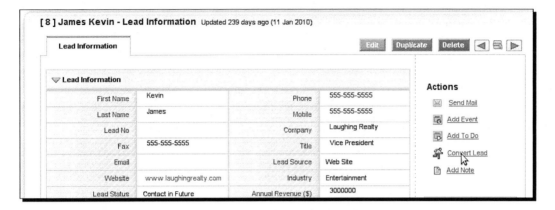

2. A pre-filled popup form will appear. Let's assume our sales process doesn't include a "potential" stage and that we want to convert Kevin and his company, Laughing Realty, into an account directly. So let's check the box labeled **Do not create a New Potential upon Conversion** and leave the rest of the fields blank. Click on **Save**:

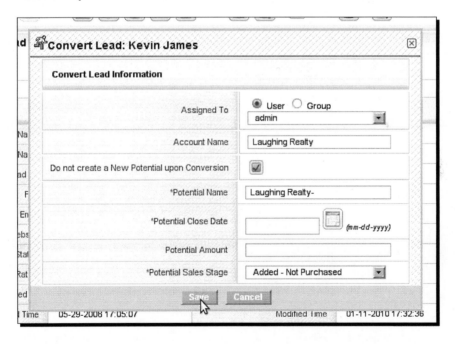

3. Up comes the Laughing Realty account page. The lead, Kevin James, has been converted into the account Laughing Realty. You can also find a new contact in the Contacts module for Kevin James:

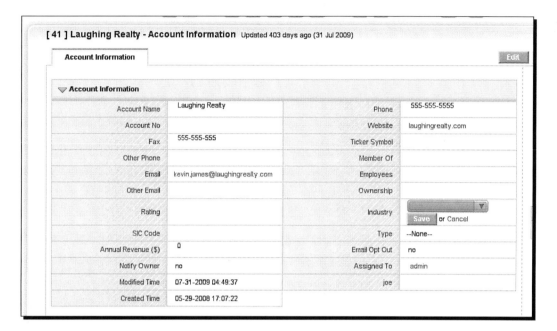

What just happened?

We just used the Actions menu list on the detail screen to convert a lead directly into an account. Now the lead displays in the Accounts module of vtiger and will show up in dashboards and reports as such.

Managing lists

Lists are a big part of managing customers and leads and just doing business in general. In this section, we'll explore how vtiger makes it easier to manage your lists, whether they be Leads, Accounts, Contacts, and so on.

The list view

The list view is another place where sales professionals will spend a big chunk of time. As the effective CRM tool that it is, vtiger has made sure that list management is a main focus.

Navigating results

The paging feature is pretty standard—you can go forward or back one page and you can skip to the first or last page of results if you want to:

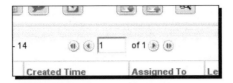

How many results are displayed?

By default, vtiger shows 20 results per page. But, you can change that by modifying the configuration file. Here's how.

Modify the `config.inc.php` file in the root of your vtiger directory and add this line anywhere in the file. Just make sure it's in between the PHP begin and end tags—`<?php` and `?>` respectively. Here is the line to add:

```
$list_max_entries_per_page = 50;
```

This would show 50 results per page.

Using Mass Edit

You can use the Mass Edit feature to change data across multiple leads at once. For example, you can assign multiple leads, accounts, or potentials to a user at one time. Here's how to do it.

Time for action – using Mass Edit to assign leads

1. In the list view, **select** the leads, potentials, or accounts that you want to assign. Click on the **Mass Edit** button:

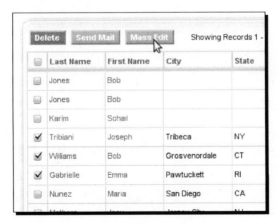

2. A popup window appears containing all of the record's fields. Now, select a user from the **Assigned To** dropdown. For example, we've selected Bob Johnson:

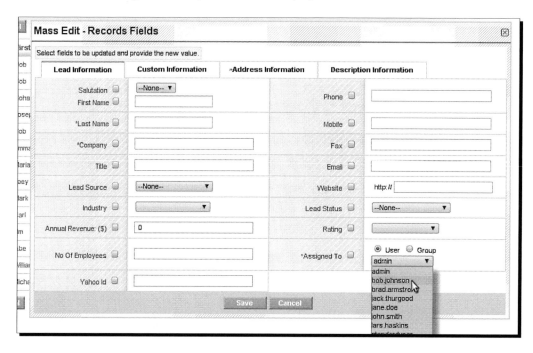

3. Now click **Save**:

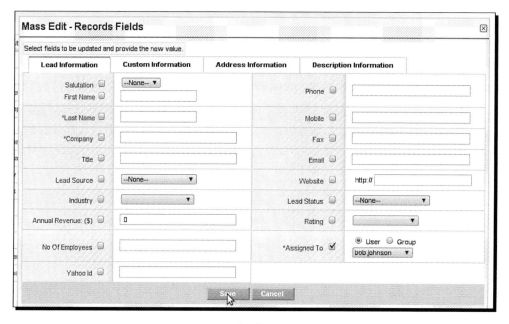

4. The selected leads are now assigned to bob.johnson:

☐	Karim	Sonan			05-19-2010 17:56:01	jane.doe	--No
☐	Tribiani	Joseph	Tribeca	NY	05-29-2008 17:05:07	bob.johnson	Cont
☐	Williams	Bob	Grosvenordale	CT	05-29-2008 17:05:08	bob.johnson	Cont
☐	Gabrielle	Emma	Pawtuckett	RI	05-29-2008 17:05:07	bob.johnson	Cont
☐	Nunez	Maria	San Diego	CA	05-29-2008 17:05:07	admin	Cont

What just happened?

We assigned multiple leads to a user by using the **Mass Edit** feature. You can use this feature to also edit any other fields in multiple leads, potentials, or accounts at once.

Using filters

Filters will allow you to look at lists of CRM records, but only a subset. For example, all leads that are assigned to a particular user or all leads that are in a particular state. Filters allow you to look at your pipeline from different perspectives.

For example you can decide which fields/columns are displayed in the list and you can also filter them based on ranges of time. Here's what the screen looks like where you create a new filter:

Time for action – creating a custom filter

While vtiger comes with several useful filters out-of-the-box, you'll get the most benefit if you create filters that are specific to your sales process. Let's assume that a sales manager wants to be able to see all the leads that were generated from a business conference. Let's create a custom filter that shows us these leads:

1. Go to **Leads** and now click on the **New** link next to the **Filters** dropdown menu:

2. On the **New Custom view** screen, let's name the view/filter **Conference Leads**. Then let's check **List in metrics** so it will show in the key metrics dashboard. Let's also check **Set as Public** so that the rest of our sales team can use the filter too. Let's choose the fields that we want to display in the view according to the following screenshot. Leave the **Simple Time Filter** section blank and then click on the **Advanced Filters** tab, where we'll set the filter to show only conference sourced leads:

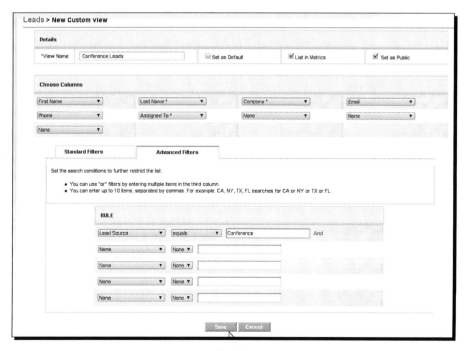

3. On the **Advanced Filters** tab, in the first drop down to the far left, choose the field. In this case, **Lead Source**. As an operator, choose **equals**. Then just fill in the value **Conference**. Click on **Save**.

4. After clicking on **Save**, you should be shown a screen, like the one below, that only shows leads that were from a conference. Of course, in order to be able to see these **Leads**, you'll have to first mark some leads in your system for having **Conference** as the **Lead Source**:

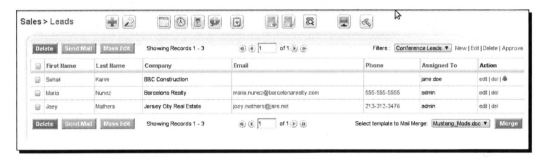

What just happened?

Using the custom filter feature in vtiger, we created a view of leads that will only show us those leads that were sourced at a conference. Now we can follow up on those conference leads easily.

Cross-linking CRM data

Tracking related data is one of the keys of good CRM. vtiger does this very well. Take a look at this screenshot of the related information section of the Loaded Pockets, Inc. account details page. You can see the related information section by scrolling down on the account detail page:

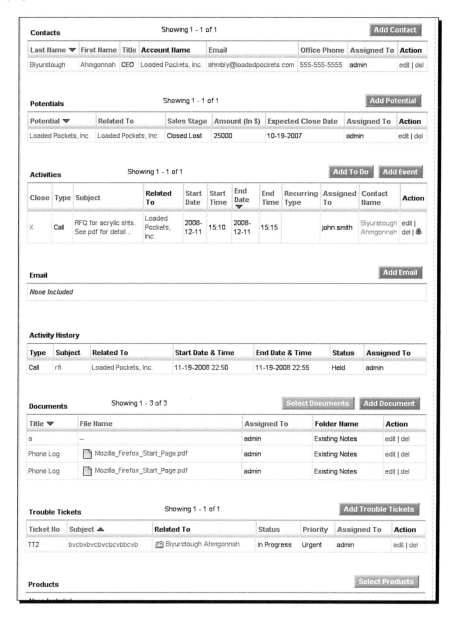

On the Account details page, you not only can see all of the pertinent account information, but you can also see all of the contacts for this Account, the Potentials, the activities on this Account, related email messages, related documents, related support/Trouble Tickets, and Products.

You can show a virtually unlimited amount of related information on a record detail page like this. You can even show information that it is in a custom module (see Chapter 10).

Each section of related information is accompanied by buttons that allow you to quickly add pieces of related information from the current detail screen, so you don't have to click into another module and create the relationship by hand.

Storing documents

The Documents module in vtiger allows you to upload file and documents and organize them into folders. This allows your organization to have one central location where critical files are stored:

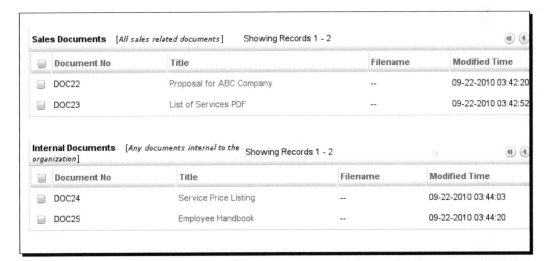

	Document No	Title	Filename	Modified Time
	DOC22	Proposal for ABC Company	--	09-22-2010 03:42:20
	DOC23	List of Services PDF	--	09-22-2010 03:42:52

	Document No	Title	Filename	Modified Time
	DOC24	Service Price Listing	--	09-22-2010 03:44:03
	DOC25	Employee Handbook	--	09-22-2010 03:44:20

Time for action – attaching an existing document to a lead

In order to follow along in this section we're going to first add a **Document** into vtiger and then take that **Document** and attach it to a **Lead**:

1. Go to **Tools | Documents** and then click on the plus sign icon.

2. Now enter a title in for your **Document**. In this example the title is **Service Price Listing**.

3. Now choose **Internal** for **Download Type** and browse to the file on your computer.

4. Click on **Save**:

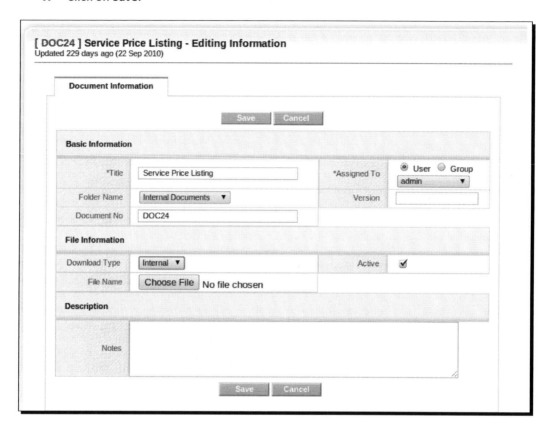

5. Now let's attach this document to a **Lead**. From the lead detail screen, scroll down to the **Documents** section and click on **Select Documents**:

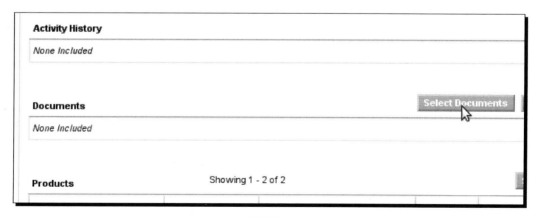

6. We want to attach the document **Service Price Listing**, so let's click on the **S** for a quick search. When the document comes up in the search, let's click on it to select it:

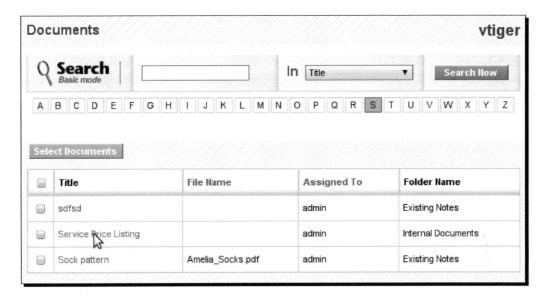

7. You will be returned to the lead detail page, and you'll see the document **Service Price Listing**, which now appears in the **Documents** section:

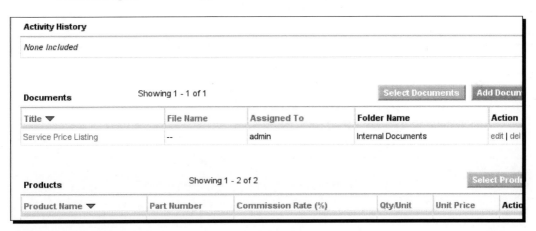

What just happened?

In a few steps we were able to find a Document already stored in vtiger and relate it to a Lead. You can follow the same steps to relate a Document to an Account, Contact, and so on.

Tracking customer communication via e-mail

With the addition of the Email module in vtiger, we're able to send emails to our leads, accounts, and contacts and we're also able to track them in vtiger. This allows us to get a clear picture of all communications with the customer.

Time for action – sending and tracking an e-mail for a lead

1. From the lead detail screen, scroll down to the **Email** section and click on **Add Email**:

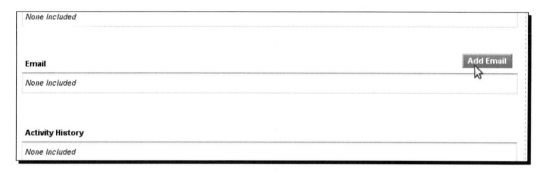

2. Or click the **Send Mail** link on the right side-bar under **Actions**:

3. On the popup selection window, make sure the customer's email address is selected and click on **Select**:

4. When the **Compose E-Mail** window opens, write your email and send it off by clicking on **Send**:

5. You'll be returned to the lead detail screen and you'll see the email you just sent to the customer in the **Email** section:

What just happened?

We successfully used vtiger's email capabilities to send an email to a customer from directly within vtiger. Now we can see it in the Email history for the lead.

Summary

In this chapter we learned quite a bit about how to use vtiger in our day-to-day operations. Specifically, we covered:

◆ The advantages of vtiger's user interface

◆ How to manage lists of leads, accounts and contacts

◆ How to cross-link or relate CRM data

◆ How to store and link documents

◆ How to track customer email communications

In the next chapter, we'll go beyond just *utilizing* vtiger's capabilities. We'll start to *expand* its capabilities by customizing layouts and fields.

5
House Training your Secret Weapon—vtiger CRM and your Business

We have spent quite a bit of time in vtiger at this point and we really know how to get around. But now it's time to give this cat some training and teach it not to destroy the house—but to destroy the competition. In this chapter, you'll learn about the customization features that vtiger offers and how to use them to create an implementation that is specific to your particular business. This will help you to keep a competitive edge.

In this chapter we shall:

◆ Learn how to use vtiger's Module Manager

◆ Add some custom fields through vtiger's Layout Editor

◆ Add some custom picklists (drop-down lists)

◆ Create some custom calculated fields

◆ Change the layout of a detail screen

What is a module?

Before we understand how to use the Module Manager in vtiger CRM, let's consider what a "module" is in vtiger.

One way to help us understand is by looking at the list of modules in the Module Manager. Log in to vtiger and go to **Settings | Module Manager** as shown in the following screenshot:

vtiger CRM handles "modules" in a similar manner to SugarCRM. Each set of functionality that is related to a certain type of data such as a lead or an account, is separated into a module. This is a basic concept of good application development and facilitates application growth and modular data interaction. The list of modules shown in the following screenshot of the Module Manager shows the list of modules in vtiger:

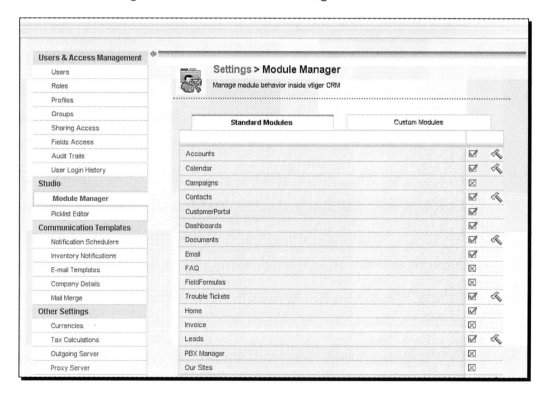

Using the module manager

Notice in the previous screenshot that there are two tabs: **Standard Modules** and **Custom Modules**.

Standard Modules are the modules that come in the vtiger core code. These modules are designed and developed by the vtiger team. However, the vtiger team may opt to put community-developed modules into the core code. Examples of the core modules are Accounts, Leads, Contacts, and so on.

Custom Modules are modules that are developed by the community and contributed. However, a private custom module can also be developed by any organization and also installed into the **Custom Modules** section of a vtiger instance. An example of a custom module is the Mobile module, which you can see in the following screenshot:

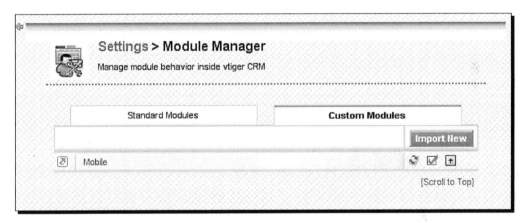

Enabling and disabling modules

You can enable any standard or custom module. When a module is enabled, a green checked box is shown. To disable that module, click the green checked box.

When a module is disabled, a red X box is shown. To enable it, just click on the red X box.

In the following screenshot, the **Accounts**, **Calendar**, and **Contacts** modules are enabled, yet the **Campaigns** module is disabled:

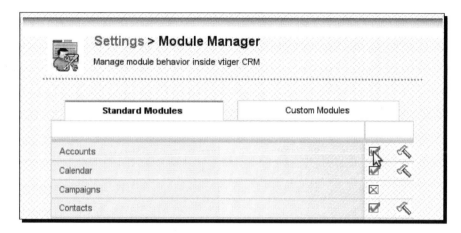

Installing a custom module

We'll explore creating our own custom modules in *Chapter 10*, but for now, let's install a commonly used module from the vtiger community. We're going to download and install Time/Material module. Here is the description of the Time/Material module from the vtiger CRM Community Website:

> *Time and Material (Timecontrol) records are relations of time, material, (products/ services), and work done during the working day that are related to the entities that consume this time and/or material. The idea is to be able to register all time spent during the working day.*

 In vtiger CRM, custom modules can be difficult to remove or uninstall. I recommend first installing them on a test or beta system and then installing them on your production server once you've done some testing and are pleased with the module's functionality.

Time for action – installing the PDF configurator module

1. Download the module. Go to the Time/Material project page here: http://forge.vtiger.com/projects/tstrcontrol.

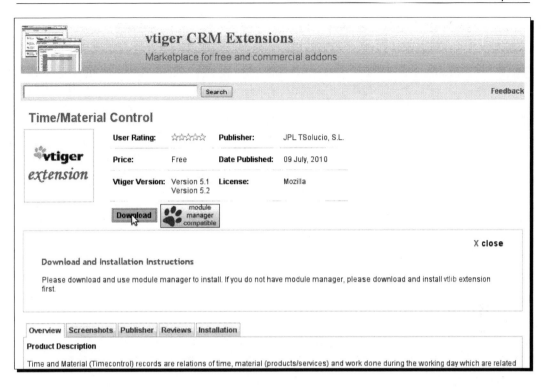

2. Download the file to your desktop for easy access.

3. Log in to vtiger CRM and go to **Settings | Module Manager**:

4. Click on **Import New**:

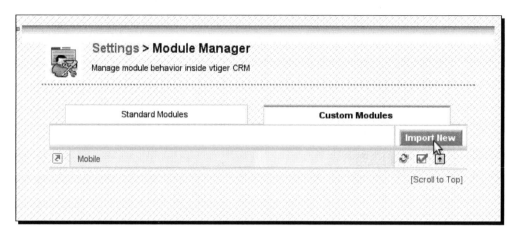

5. On the next screen, click on **Choose File**:

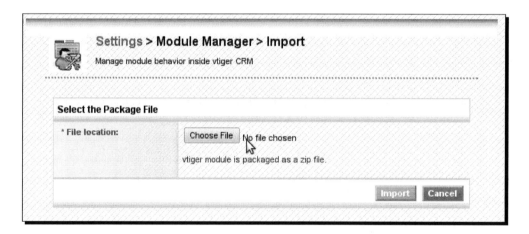

6. Browse to your desktop and choose the file **Timecontrol510-1.zip**.

7. Now click the **Import** button back in vtiger:

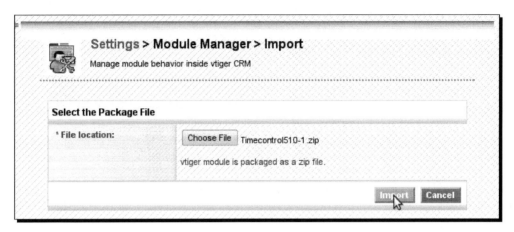

8. On the next screen you'll be asked if you want to proceed with the import. Click on **Yes**.

9. On the next screen, you should see a list of status messages showing the successful installation of the Time/Material module:

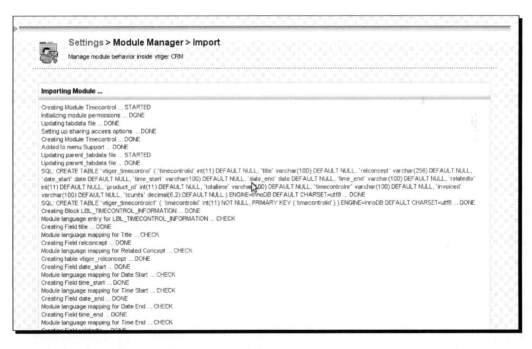

10. To complete the installation, click on **Finish**.

What just happened?

We successfully installed a module into vtiger CRM using the Module Manager.

Let's see what else we can do with Module Manager!

Creating custom fields

Custom fields will allow you to include CRM data that is specific to your particular business or industry. For example, if your company sells alcoholic beverages, you can track a customer contact's favorite beverage so you can send them a gift once in a while. Let's create a custom field.

Time for action – creating custom fields

1. Log in to vtiger CRM and go to **Settings | Module Manager**:

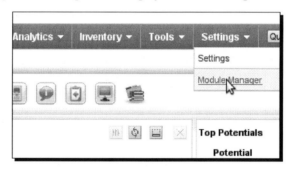

2. Now, scroll down and click on the little hammer icon for the **Contacts** module. That will open the **Contacts** module settings page.

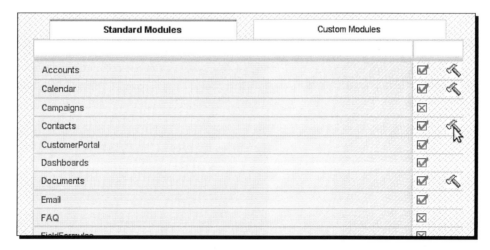

3. On the next screen, click on **Layout Editor**:

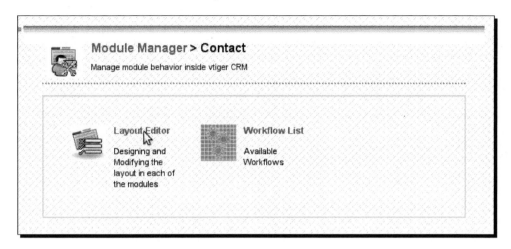

4. On the next screen, click on the little blue plus sign in the title bar of the **Contact Information** block:

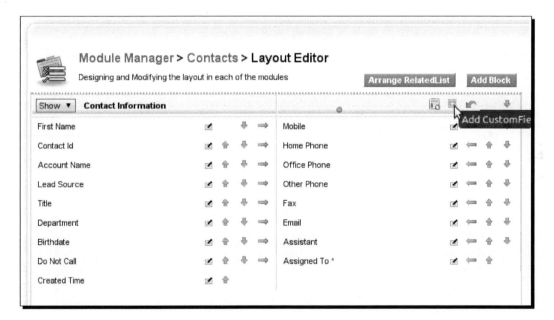

5. On the screen that pops up, enter in the label **Favorite Beverage**, choose the field type to the left, **Text**, and then let's enter a field length of **25**. Click on **Save**:

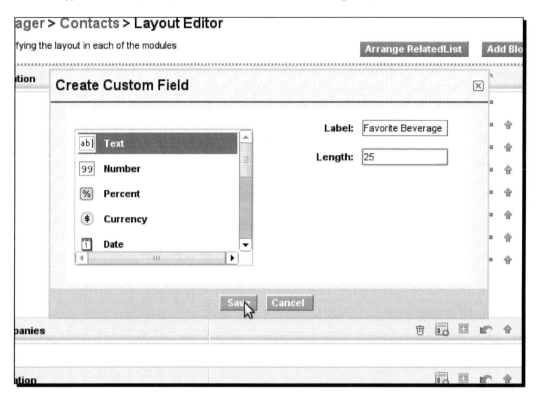

6. Now, you can see the field **Favorite Beverage** at the end of the field list:

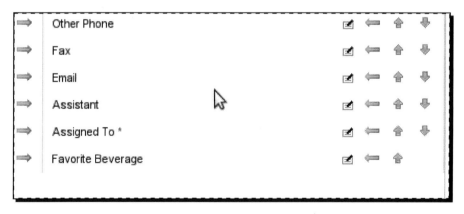

7. Now let's test it out. Go to a contact in the **Contacts** section. We can see the field there and we can enter something so that we know that Patricia Johnson likes **Absolute Mandarin**:

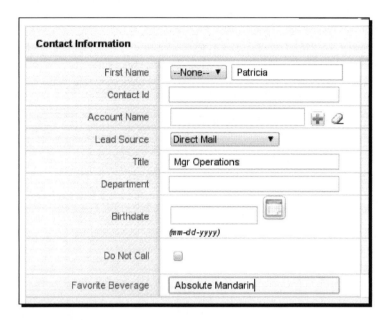

What just happened?

We used vtiger's Module Manager to create a custom field that tracks the customer's favorite beverage. We went into the Contacts module's **Settings** screen and used Module Manager's Layout Editor to add a custom field.

Have a go hero

There are many other types of custom fields that you can add, such as **text**, **number**, **email**, **phone**, **date**, **URL**, **checkbox**, and even a **Skype** username. Using the **Layout Editor** in **Module Manager**, try to add your own custom fields.

Creating custom drop-down menus

What if you don't want to create a single entry field? What if you want to create a custom dropdown menu? Once again, we can use vtiger's Module Manager. Vtiger uses the term **pick list** to refer to dropdown menus. Let's create the same field—**Favorite Beverage**—but let's make it a dropdown menu.

Time for action – creating a custom pick list (Drop-down menu)

1. Log in to vtiger CRM and go to **Settings | Module Manager**:

2. Now, scroll down and click on the little hammer icon for the **Contacts** module. That will open the **Contacts** module settings page.

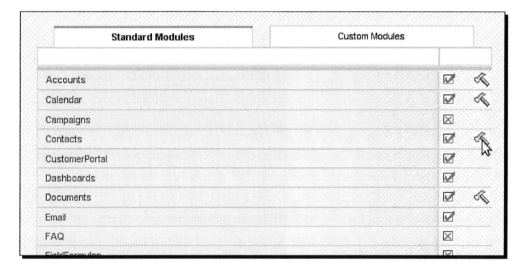

3. On the next screen, click on **Layout Editor**:

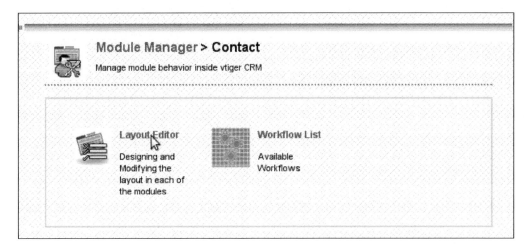

4. On the next screen, click on the little blue plus sign in the title bar of the **Contact Information** block:

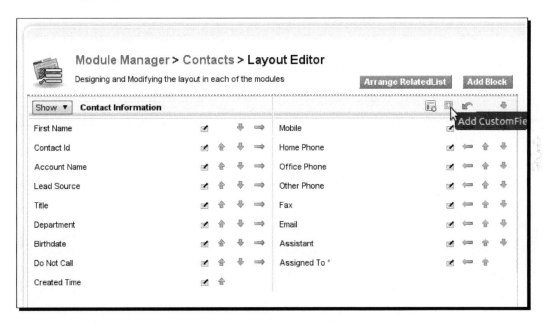

5. On the screen that pops up, enter in the label **Favorite Beverage**, choose the field type to the left, **Text**, and then let's enter a field length of **25**. Click on **Save**:

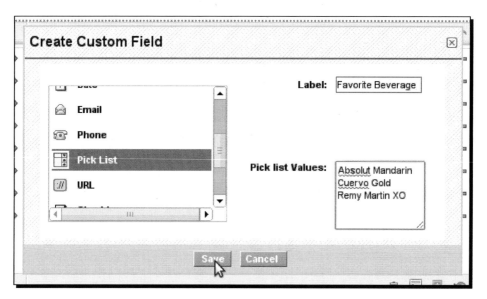

6. Now, you can see the field **Favorite Beverage** at the end of the field list:

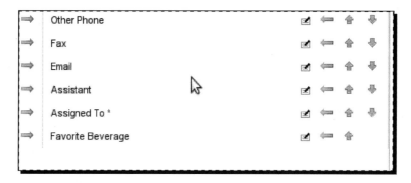

7. Now let's test it out. Go to a contact in the **Contacts** section. We can now see the dropdown list there and we can add a beverage:

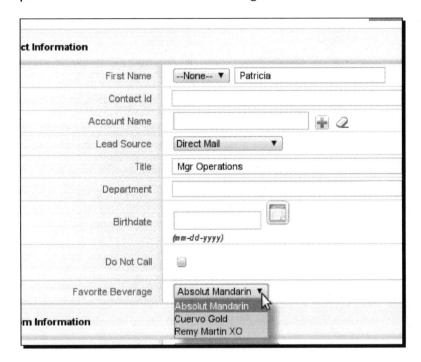

What just happened?

We used Module Manager once again to create a custom field, but this time, we created a **pick list** (dropdown menu) with our own custom values.

Custom calculated fields

What is a custom calculated field in vtiger CRM? A custom calculated field allows you to create a field value for a lead, account, and so on that will be calculated based on other fields. For instance, many sales people are used to seeing a weighted potential value for potential sales.

This is usually calculated as probability X potential amount. So, if a potential sale has a probability of 80 percent and is for $100,000 then the weighted value would be $80,000. This helps sales people to prioritize the leads they're working on.

So, let's create this "weighted value" field in vtiger.

Time for action – creating a custom calculated field

1. Log in to vtiger CRM and go to **Settings | Module Manager**:

2. Now click the hammer icon for the **Potentials** module to enter into the settings area for the **Potentials** module:

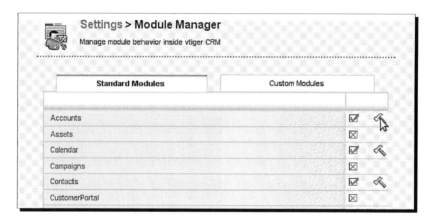

3. Now click on **Field Formulas**:

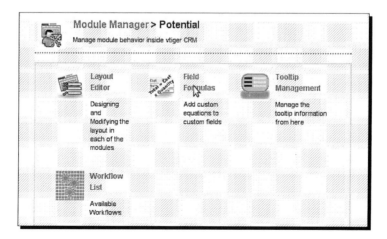

4. You need to have a custom field in a module before you can create a calculated field. Therefore, you can see a message stating that and a link to **Custom field**. Click on it:

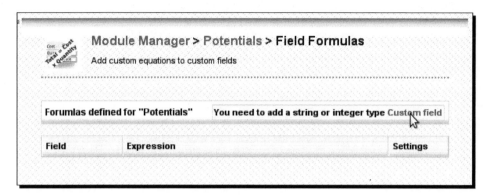

5. This will bring you to the **Layout Editor** screen. Click the blue plus sign to create your custom field:

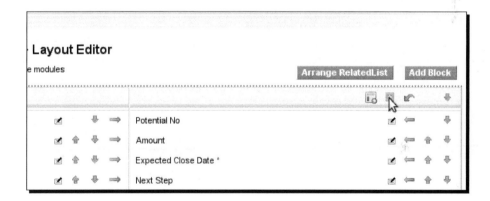

6. On the next screen that pops up, choose the field **Number**, and then call the field **Weighted Value**. Make it **10** characters long and give it **2** decimal places. Click on **Save**:

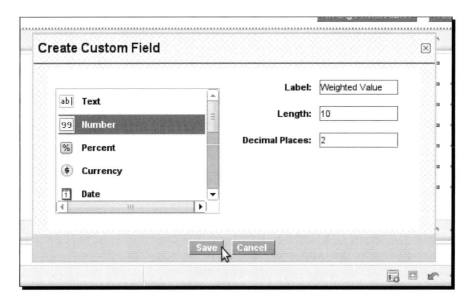

7. You can now see the **Weighted Value** field in the field list. Now go back to the **Module Manager** screen for the Potentials module by clicking on **Potentials** in the breadcrumb link:

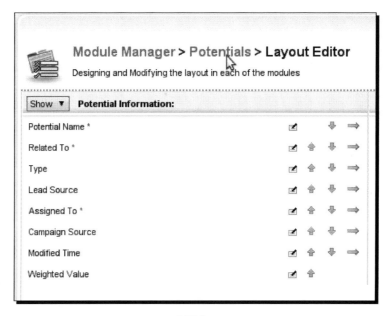

8. Now, click on **Field Formulas**:

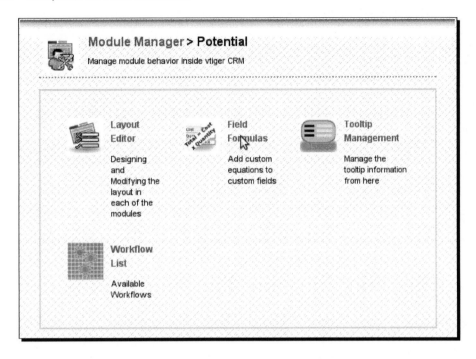

9. Now the button **New Field Expression** is available. Click it:

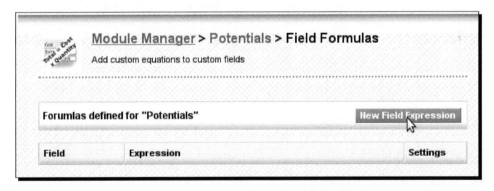

10. On the screen that pops up, you can see your only custom field—**Weighted Value**—already selected in the **Target Field** box:

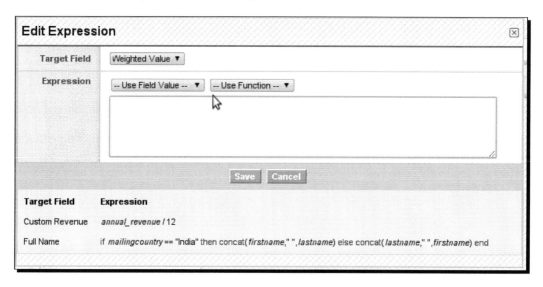

11. Now, in the expression area, choose the Probability field from the box labeled **--Use Field Value--**:

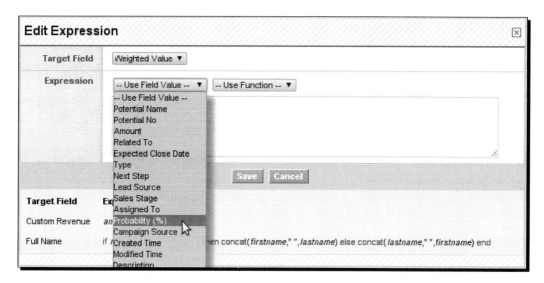

12. After the field name **probability** appears to start the formula, now divide it by **100** to get the percentage expressed as a fraction. Also put parentheses around it since we're going to use the result in another part of the equation:

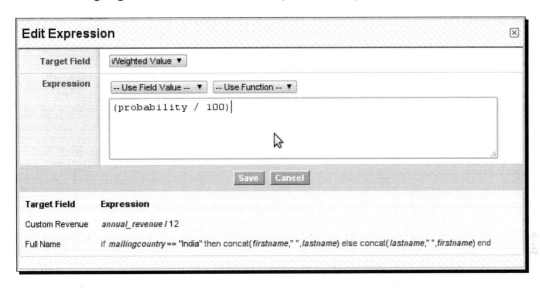

13. Now, multiply that by the **Amount** field by typing a * after the probability fraction conversion and choose the **Amount** field from the --**Use Field Value**-- box:

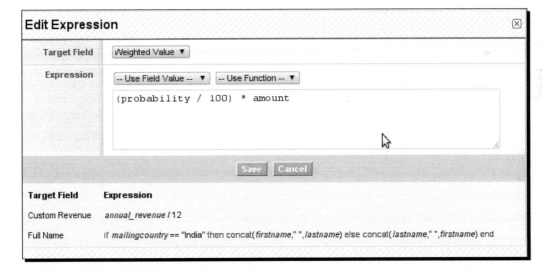

14. We're done! Click on **Save**.

15. Now let's go to a **Potential** and make sure the **Probability** and **Amount** fields are filled in. We can see the **Weighted Value** of the potential sale:

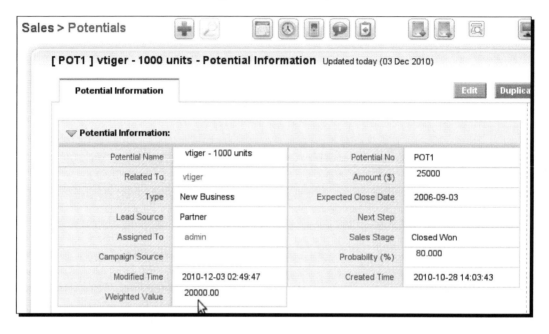

What just happened?

We used Module Manager's calculated field feature to create a field called Weighted Value. The custom field is a calculated value based on the values of the Probability and Amount fields for a potential. The formula is: probability x amount = weighted value.

Changing the layout of the fields

So now you've got all of your custom fields, custom dropdowns, and custom calculated fields in vtiger CRM. But now you want to change the order that they're listed in for easy, quick access to the most important information.

With the Layout Editor, we can do just that. Let's take a moment first to consider how vtiger CRM organizes the layout for CRM entities.

Blocks

A block is a section on the page that holds a group of fields, usually by the type of information. For instance, on the potential screen, the very first block is called **Potential Information**. This block displays the most important information for the potential:

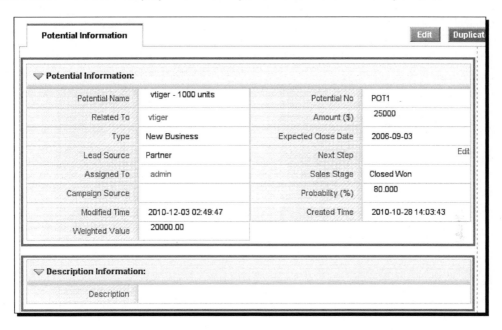

Then there is also a **Description Block** which holds only the **Description** field by default.

Related Lists

A Related List is a list of related CRM entities. For example, in the Potentials module, a related list is the **Contacts** list. The **Activities** list is another example:

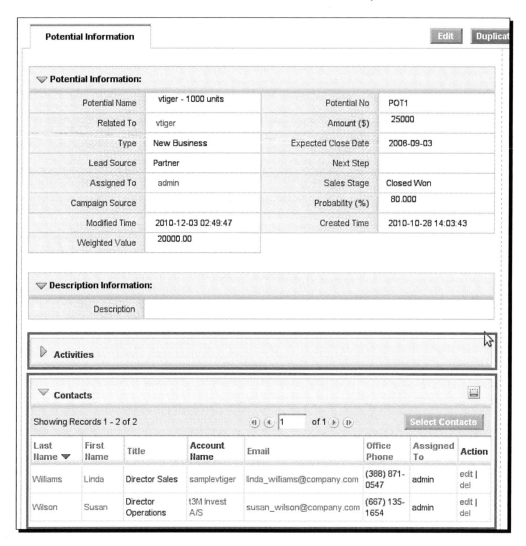

Now that we understand the different elements of the layout, let's change it around to our liking.

Time for action – changing the Layout

1. Log in to vtiger CRM and go to **Settings | Module Manager**:

2. Now, scroll down and click the hammer icon to enter the Module Manager for the **Potentials Module**:

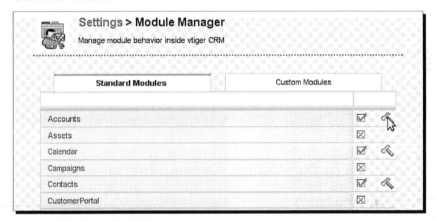

3. Now click on the **Layout Editor**:

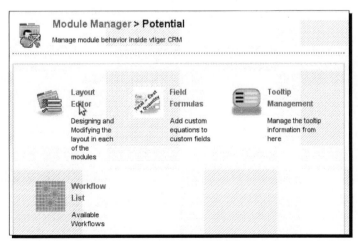

4. On the **Layout Editor** screen, use the different **arrows** to move fields and blocks:

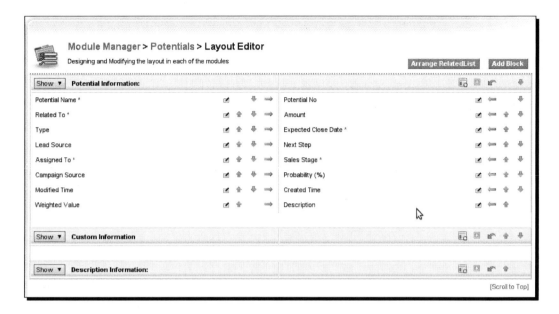

5. Let's move the **Probability**, **Amount**, and **Weighted Value** fields all to the upper area of the right column, since they're all related. Just click the arrows to move the fields around until they are in the right position:

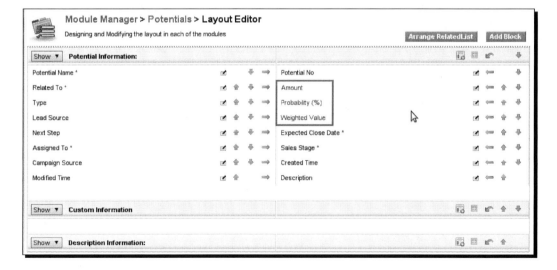

6. Now let's change the order of the Related Lists. To do this, just click on the **Arrange RelatedList** button:

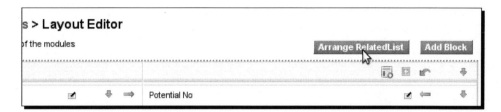

7. On the screen that pops up, once again use the arrows to shift the position of the related lists:

8. When you're done, just click the **X** button to close the window. When you're done with all of your changes, there's no need to save. Just return to the potential to see your implemented changes:

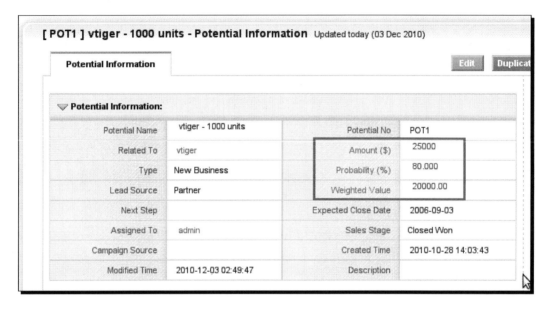

What just happened?

You changed the layout of the potentials screen. We used the Layout Editor to change the position of three fields—Probability, Amount, and Weighted Value in the Potentials module. Since they're all related fields, we put them together in the interface.

You can go through these same steps to modify the layout in any of the modules.

Summary

In this chapter, we learned how to customize vtiger CRM—how to use Module Manager. Specifically we covered:

◆ How to create custom fields

◆ How to create custom dropdown menus with the Picklist Editor

◆ How to create custom calculated fields with Field Formulas

◆ How to change the layout of CRM entity screens with the Layout Editor

In the next chapter, we'll learn how to take your company's unique business processes and manage them in vtiger CRM.

6

Business Processes—They're G-r-r-r-reat!

*Everyone dreams of sitting back, flipping a few switches and watching your business grow. I know that when we started aimtheory, (*www.aimtheory.com*) that is exactly what we were aspiring for, since our values are built around reaching those kinds of goals.*

While vtiger doesn't actually make this dream come true, it can really take the weight off by automating some simple business processes. In this chapter, we're going to continue the theme of customization and you will learn how to utilize vtiger's automation capabilities. We're going to discover what workflow is in vtiger CRM, how we can automate steps in your processes and map custom fields to flow through them.

In this chapter we'll cover:

- ◆ Mapping custom fields
- ◆ What is a workflow?
- ◆ How to create a workflow in vtiger CRM
    - ❑ Setting up the Workflow module with a third-party
    - ❑ Setting up the Workflow module in Windows
    - ❑ Setting up the Workflow module in Linux
- ◆ Creating a workflow
- ◆ Advanced workflow
    - ❑ Using custom code in a workflow

Mapping custom fields

In Chapter 5, we created custom fields that are specific to your business model and processes. However, while you may have created custom fields in the **Leads** module, we want to make sure that the custom data stays with that particular customer as they flow through the sales process to **Potential** and then become an **Account**.

Time for action – mapping custom fields

Let's map the custom fields that we created in the leads module through to Potentials and Accounts:

1. The first thing you'll have to do is make sure that you have created custom fields in the Leads, Potentials, and Accounts modules with the same names and field types. For help in doing this, see Chapter 5.

2. Log in to vtiger CRM and go to **Settings | Module Manager**:

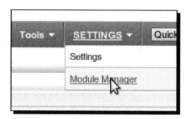

3. Now click the hammer icon (for settings) next to the Leads module:

4. Now click **Leads Custom Field Mapping**:

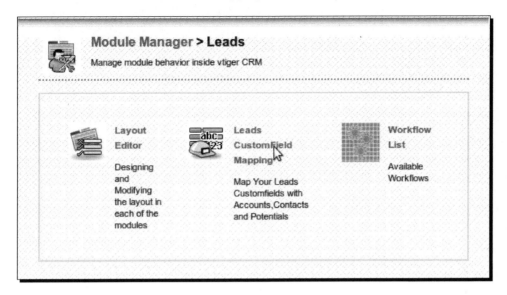

5. On the next screen, you are shown the settings for each of your custom fields. We're going to map a field called **Custom Text Field**. Click on **Edit** to change these settings:

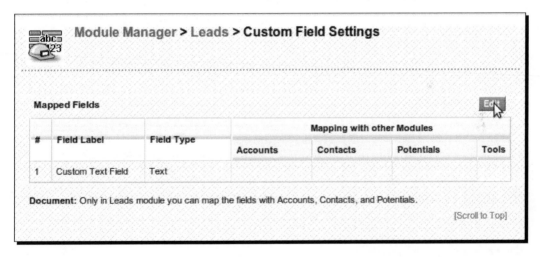

6. We're going to map the field between modules on this screen. Just use the dropdown boxes to choose the field **Custom Text Field** in each module. Click on **Save** to save the mapping:

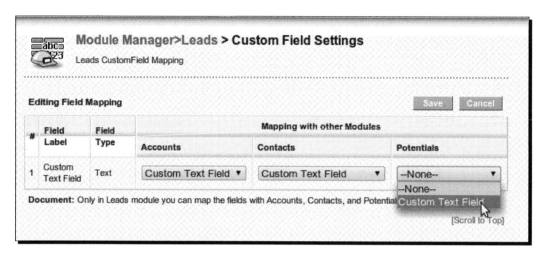

7. Now the field is mapped. It will carry through all business processes:

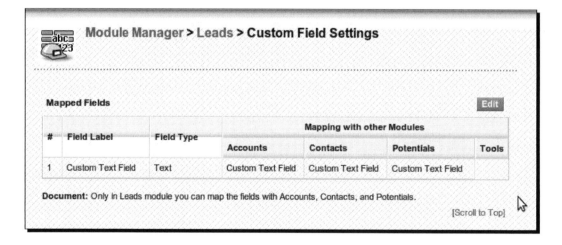

What just happened?

We used Module Manager to map a custom field between the Leads, Contacts, and Potentials modules. Now when data is entered into the custom field **Custom Text Field**, it will carry through as it is converted into a Lead, Account, and the Contact that is related to the Account.

What is a workflow?

Well let's first take a look at how Wikipedia defines it (en.wikipedia.org/wiki/Workflow) and then we'll dumb it down a bit:

> *A workflow consists of a sequence of connected steps. It is a depiction of a sequence of operations, declared as work of a person, a group of persons, an organization of staff, or one or more simple or complex mechanisms. The flow being described often refers to a document that is being transferred from one step to another.*

Workflows allow us to focus on business processes and make them more efficient. In vtiger CRM, workflows will allow us to control and automate the flow of information between people and/or between steps in a business process.

What is an example of a workflow? Let's say that you want to send a thank you message out each time you win a new customer. What happens in vtiger CRM? A Lead or a Potential is converted to an account and is saved for the first time. When that first save takes place, vtiger sends an email to the customer using a predefined email template.

How about another? Bob Johnson is assigned a new lead. You want to make sure that he'll begin the sales process with that lead, so you want to assign him a To-Do so he'll make sure to contact them. What happens in vtiger CRM? The first time the lead is saved, a To-Do is created automatically for Bob Johnson and he receives a popup reminder with an option to send an email as well.

How to create a workflow in vtiger CRM

First things first. In order for workflow to flow, you first need to set up a cron service. A cron service runs every so often on a schedule that you specify and tell vtiger to perform the automated tasks that you set up.

Here's how to do it with:

- A third party cron service provider
- In Windows
- Linux

For the second and third points you'll need to perform these steps on the computer that is hosting vtiger CRM.

Time for action – setting up the workflow module with a third-party

As an alternative to setting up Windows or Linux to run the cron service, you can get several online free services like `setcronjob.com` or `cronless.com`. However, in order to use these services your vtiger CRM server needs to be hosted somewhere online.

How does it work? Basically, you tell those services what URL to ping every so often on a schedule that you specify. When setting up the service just give them the following URL to set up workflow in vtiger CRM:

```
http://[YOUR DOMAIN NAME HERE]/vtigercron.php?service=com_vtiger_
workflow&app_key=[YOUR APP KEY HERE]
```

Just make sure to change this URL to include your own domain name where vtiger CRM is hosted and your app key. How do you get your app key?

1. Open the file `config.inc.php` in the root of your vtiger CRM directory.

2. Find the following line of code:
   ```
   // Generating Unique Application Key
   $application_unique_key = '[YOUR KEY IS A LONG STRING VALUE
   HERE]';
   ```

3. Now paste your app key into the URL and provide it to the third-party cron service.

4. The third-party service will now ensure that your workflow script is run regularly at the interval that you have set.

What just happened?

We just configured the workflows in vtiger CRM to be run on a time schedule using a third-party cron service. The third-party service will call the cron script in vtiger on a schedule and process vtiger's workflows.

Time for action – setting up the workflow module in Windows

For the workflow module to work properly in Windows:

◆ The workflow script must be modified and

◆ A scheduled task must be set up using the Scheduled Task tool in Control Panel.

These instructions assume that you have used the Windows installer to install vtiger CRM. If you installed it from source, then you will have to modify the file locations in the `com_vtiger_workflow.bat` file. To modify the workflow script:

1. Open the file `cron/modules/com_vtiger_workflow/com_vtiger_workflow.bat` in the root of the vtigercrm directory. Here's what the file should look like:

    ```
    set VTIGERCRM_ROOTDIR=" Files\vtigercrm5\apache\htdocs\C:\
    ProgramvtigerCRM"

    set PHP_EXE="C:\Program Files\vtigercrm5\php\php.exe"

    cd /D %VTIGERCRM_ROOTDIR%

    %PHP_EXE% -f vtigercron.php service="com_vtiger_workflow" app_
    key="YOUR_APP_KEY_HERE"
    ```

2. Make sure that the paths are pointing to the right places and modify them if you need to.

3. Now get your vtiger CRM app key. Open the file `config.inc.php` in the root of your vtiger CRM directory.

4. Find the following line of code:

    ```
    // Generating Unique Application Key
    $application_unique_key = '[YOUR KEY IS A LONG STRING VALUE
    HERE]';
    ```

5. Copy the long value of the variable `$application_unique_key`.

6. Now go back to the `com_vtiger_workflow.bat` file and find the line with the following code:

    ```
    %PHP_EXE% -f vtigercron.php service="com_vtiger_workflow" app_
    key="YOUR_APP_KEY_HERE"
    ```

7. Insert your app key where it says `YOUR_APP_KEY_HERE`. Make sure you leave the quotes.

8. Save the changes and close the file.

9. Now you need to set up the scheduled task in Windows.

10. Open **Control Panel**.

11. Open **Scheduled Tasks**.

12. Create a new scheduled task called **vtiger CRM cron**.

13. Indicate that you want the task to recur **Daily**.

14. Then, using the **Schedule** tab, click on **Advanced** and indicate the interval that you want it to repeat. Set it to every minute if you'd like all automation to occur in near real time.

15. Save the scheduled task.

What just happened?

We just configured the workflows in vtiger CRM to be run on a time schedule using the Windows Task Scheduler service. The Task Scheduler service will call the cron script in vtiger on a schedule and process vtiger's workflows.

Time for action – setting up the workflow module in Linux

For the Workflow module to work properly in Linux:

◆ The Linux-based script needs to be modified

◆ The cron system in Linux must be configured properly

 This section assumes that you have installed vtiger CRM on a Linux system as described in Chapter 2 and that vtiger CRM is installed at /var/www/vtigercrm.

1. Open the file cron/modules/com_vtiger_workflow/com_vtiger_workflow. sh.

2. Here's what it should look like:

```
export VTIGERCRM_ROOTDIR=`dirname "$0"`/../../..
export USE_PHP=php

cd $VTIGERCRM_ROOTDIR

$USE_PHP -f vtigercron.php service="com_vtiger_workflow" app_
key="YOUR_APP_KEY_HERE"
```

3. Now get your vtiger CRM app key. Open the file config.inc.php in the root of your vtiger CRM directory.

4. Find the following line of code:

```
// Generating Unique Application Key
$application_unique_key = '[YOUR KEY IS A LONG STRING VALUE
HERE]';
```

5. Copy the long value of the variable `$application_unique_key`.

6. Now go back to the `com_vtiger_workflow.sh` file, and replace `YOUR_APP_KEY_HERE` with the long string value you copied from `config.inc.php`. Remember to leave the quotes.

7. Save the changes and close the file.

8. Now to set up the cron job in Linux.

9. Run the following command from a command prompt. This command will process the cron script every minute:

```
sudo crontab -l; echo "* * * * * /var/www/vtigercrm/cron/modules/
com_vtiger_workflow" | crontab
```

10. Your cron job is now saved.

 For more information on cron commands, such as how to run them every hour or every 15 minutes, please see `http://en.wikipedia.org/wiki/Cron`.

What just happened?

Without the cron service set up, some things in vtiger's Workflow module would not work properly. Now that it is configured, the Workflow module is ready to automate your business processes!

Creating a workflow

Now that the Workflow module has been configured, let's try to create a workflow. Let's go back to our two examples:

◆ **Thank You note**: Let's say that you want to send a thank you message out each time that you win a new customer. What happens in vtiger CRM? A Lead or a Potential is converted to an account and is saved for the first time. When that first save takes place, vtiger sends an email to the customer using a predefined email template.

◆ **Introductory Call Reminder**: Bob Johnson is assigned a new lead. You want to make sure that he'll begin the sales process with that lead, so you want to assign him a To-Do so he'll make sure to contact them. What happens in vtiger CRM? The first time the lead is saved, a To-Do is created automatically for Bob Johnson and he receives a popup reminder and an email as well reminding him to make that first call to the new lead.

Time for action – creating a workflow: thank you note

Let's start with example #1—the thank you note.

 For more information on cron commands, such as how to run them every hour or every 15 minutes, please see http://en.wikipedia.org/wiki/Cron.

1. In vtiger CRM, go to **Settings**:

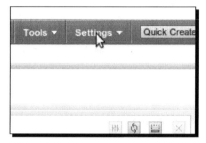

2. Now click on **Workflows**:

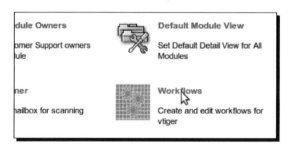

3. Click on the **New Workflow** button:

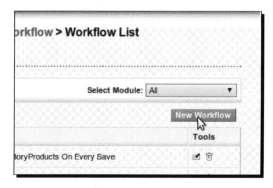

4. When the **Create Workflow** popup box opens, choose **For Module** and **Create a workflow for Accounts**. Click on **Create**:

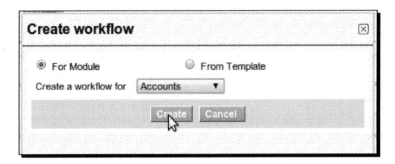

5. On the next screen enter the **Description, Send Thank You Note**. Choose to run the workflow every time the record is saved. Now click on **Save** to go to the next step:

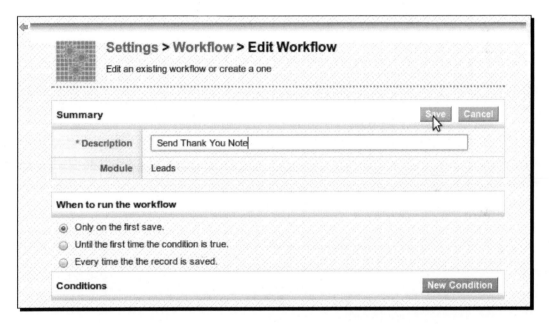

6. After you click on **Save**, the **Tasks** section appears at the bottom. This is where you'll set up the sending of the thank you note. Now click on **New Task**. We won't add any conditions here since this is an unconditional workflow. We'll deal with conditions soon enough.

7. When the **Create Task** popup box opens, choose **Send Email** and click on **Create**:

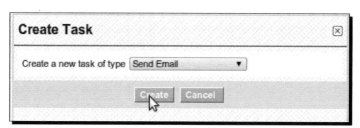

8. This will now bring you to the **Edit Task** screen. Let's name the task **Send Thank You Note** so it matches up nicely with our workflow name. Leave it marked as **Active**. We don't need to delay this task so don't check the box marked **Execute the task after some delay**. In the **Recipient** field, choose **Email** from the dropdown. This will insert the email variable into the **Recipient** field. Above the email message box, there is a dropdown that makes all of the **Account** module's fields available to you. Just choose the **First Name** field from the dropdown and it will get inserted into the text box for you. Now type your message and click the **Save** button:

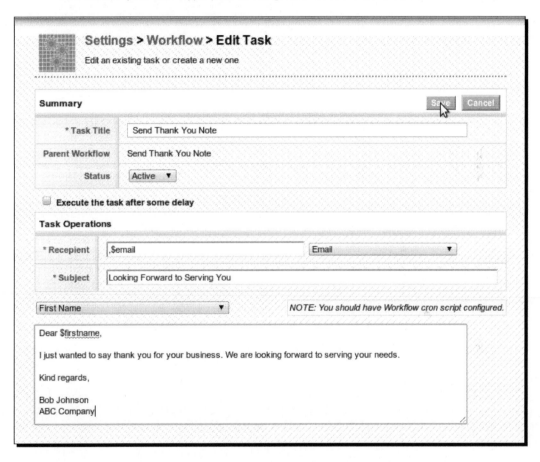

 You can also insert the user's signature automatically by using the vtiger CRM module variable $users-signature$.

9. You have saved the task related to this workflow, but you haven't yet saved the workflow. You are now returned to the **Edit Workflow** screen and you can see your new task listed. Now click on **Save** to save your new workflow:

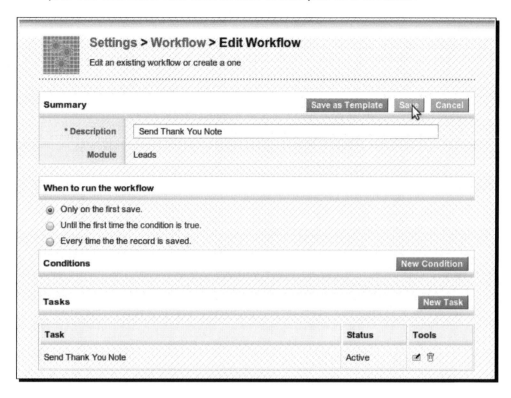

10. To test it, create an account and put your own email address in the email field of the new account. Once it's saved, you'll receive a thank you note.

What just happened?

We successfully created a workflow that will now automate thank you emails to new customers. Each time a new account is created or converted from a lead, the new customer will receive an email thanking them for their business.

Currently, vtiger CRM will process this workflow each time the account record is saved. If you want this to run only on the first save, choose the **Only on the First Save** option in step 6 of the previous exercise.

Now let's move on to example #2.

Time for action – creating a workflow: Introductory call reminder

Now we're going to a little more with workflows—we're going to create a task as a result of a lead assignment:

1. From within the **Workflows** module, click on **New Workflow**:

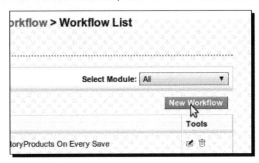

2. Choose to create a workflow for the **Leads** module:

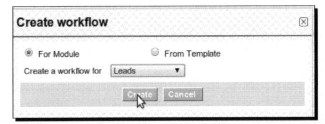

3. Let's call this workflow **Introductory Phone Call**. Let's run it **Only on the first save**. Click on **Save** to continue:

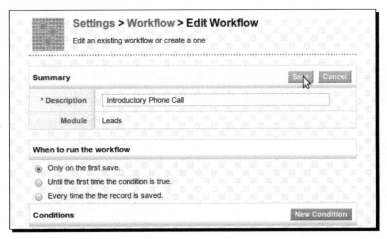

4. On the next screen, click on **New Task** to create the **Todo**:

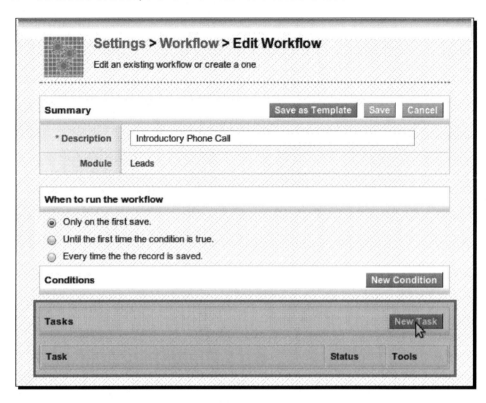

5. When the **Create Task** popup window opens, choose **Create Todo** and click on **Create**:

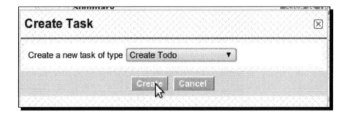

6. Let's name the task **Start the Sales Process** and give the **Todo** the subject of **First Customer Phone Call**. Give it a **Description** too. Set it for 1 day after it's created and send a notification. Click on **Save**:

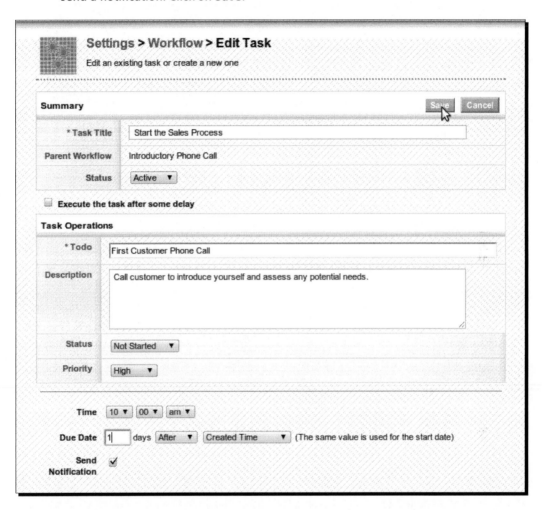

7. OK, you've saved the task that creates the **Todo**, so now save the workflow by clicking **Save** on the next screen:

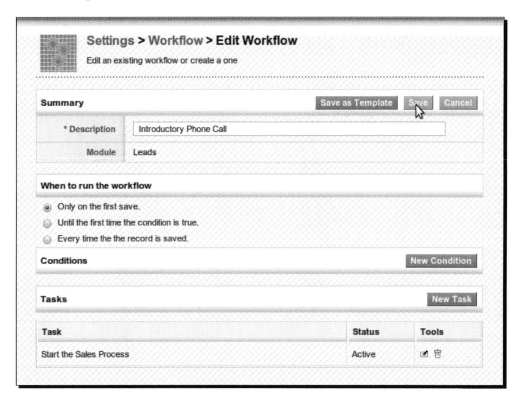

8. Now you can test it by creating a new lead and assigning it to yourself. You should see a popup reminder on the following day at 10 A.M. and also receive an email.

What just happened?

We created a workflow using vtiger CRM's workflow module. We automated the creation of a To-Do task assigned to a salesperson. It will be created when a new lead is assigned to them. They'll then get reminded through a popup and through a notification email.

Advanced workflow

Now that we've tested the waters a bit, let's do something a bit more involved. We may want to automate certain processes, but only "if" something else is true. Here enters our good old friend, "if...then". How do we do that in vtiger CRM? Let's create a conditional workflow.

First, let's establish our real world scenario/process. Let's suppose that you want to be alerted each time potentially big business walks through the door. Well, how do you define big business?

We'll do it in vtiger using a condition based on the potential amount. So, when Bob Johnson fills out the Amount field, as he's adding a new potential into the system, we'll get alerted if it's an unusually large opportunity. We'll even be able to send an alert when he makes subsequent changes. For instance, he may add the opportunity without filling out the Amount field and save it, but then he fills out the Amount field the next day during a conversation with the prospect.

Time for action – creating a conditional workflow

1. From within the **Workflows** module, click **New Workflow**:

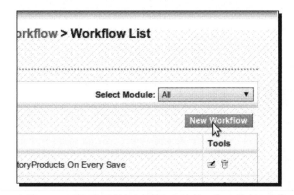

2. Let's create a workflow for the **Potentials** module:

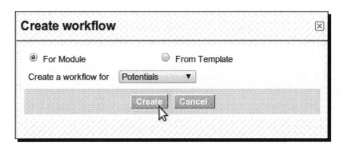

3. Let's call this workflow **Big Business Alert** and let's run it **Every time the record is saved**. This will allow us to capture subsequent changes even after the first time the record is created. Now click on **New Condition**:

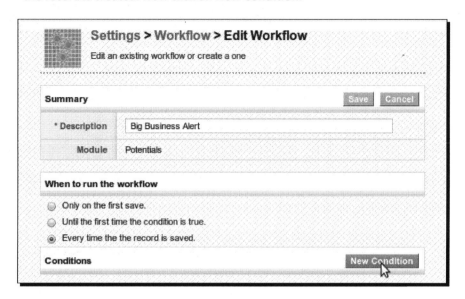

4. Choose the **Amount** field from the field list drop down and choose greater than or equal to from the operator drop down. Then fill in the amount. What's "big business"? Let's say a million bucks. Enter **1000000**. Then click on **Save**:

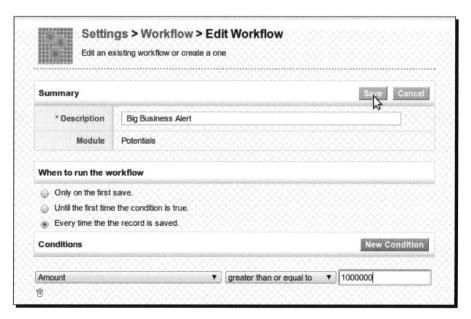

5. Now that we've saved our condition, let's add the task that will send the email. Click on **New Task**:

6. In the **Create Task** popup window, choose **Send Email** and click on **Create**:

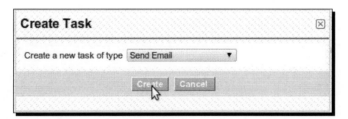

7. Let's name this task **Big Business Alert Email**. For the recipient, put in the name of the sales manager, who would want to be informed. Let's pretend you are the manager in this case, so put your own email address in for testing purposes. For the subject line, enter ***BIG BUSINESS ALERT***. Now type the email that you'd like to send. To insert the field variables shown in the image below, just choose them from the field list dropdown menu and then copy and paste them into the message where you want. Click on **Save**:

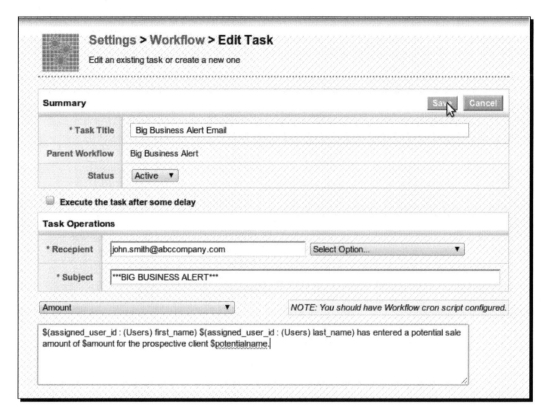

8. Now your condition and your task are both saved. Let's now save the workflow by clicking on **Save**:

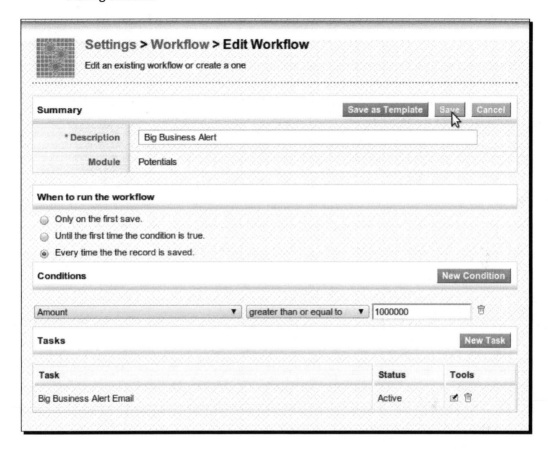

9. Now, to test, create a potential with an Amount value of 2,000,000 and save it. Assuming that Bob Johnson is the user that created the potential and ACME, Co. is the prospect, you should receive an email that looks like this:

Subject: ***BIG BUSINESS ALERT***

Bob Johnson has entered a potential sale amount of $2000000 for the prospective client ACME, Co.

What just happened?

Not only did we create a conditional workflow using conditions in vtiger CRM's workflow module, but we also sent an automated email message that contains CRM record data by using field variables.

Now try your hand at some more complicated conditions using different modules, operators, and field variables.

Using custom code in a workflow

While writing custom vtiger CRM code is beyond the scope of this book (we get into it a little bit in Chapter 10), you can run your own custom code in workflow.

When you create a workflow task and you have the dropdown list of the different task types, you also have the option **Invoke Custom Function**. Choose that option to use your custom vtiger code:

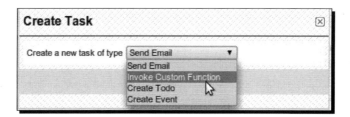

Summary

By now, you should be feeling like a pro in vtiger CRM. In this chapter, we mapped custom fields to flow through our business processes and we created workflows to automate communications and task assignments. Here's the rundown of what we covered in this chapter:

◆ How you can map custom fields to flow throughout the sales process

◆ What a Workflow is in vtiger CRM

◆ How to create a workflow in vtiger CRM

◆ How to create a conditional workflow in vtiger CRM

In the next chapter, you'll see how you can further extend vtiger CRM's capabilities by using **extensions**.

7
Super Tiger—Using vtiger Extensions

Any good software package—whether open our closed source—would be able to integrate and/or connect with other external systems and be extensible. In line with this paradigm, vtiger CRM offers both. In their "marketplace" at vtiger.com, *you'll find many add-ons that extend vtiger's functionality and allow it to integrate with other popular tools.*

For instance, email is an integral part of CRM. Sales people spend most of their days composing, reading, and replying to emails to and from their customers and prospects. It is a huge time saver to be able to track all of your emails to and from one particular client in one place.

Extensions like the ones for Mozilla Thunderbird and Microsoft Outlook make this possible and reduce the need to enter data twice or the need to shift through the hundreds of emails that some sales people get every day.

Another example has to do with customization. There is limited ability to customize the PDF invoices and quotes in vtiger CRM. You can do it, but it requires a fair amount of effort and programming know how. However, with the PDF configurator extension, you can easily customize the PDFs in various ways.

Extensions are one of the several ways that you can make vtiger your own—make it fit your organization's modus operandi.

In this chapter, we will discuss:

- ◆ The vtiger CRM extenstion community
- ◆ How to install vtiger CRM extensions
- ◆ Some useful vtiger CRM extensions

The vtiger CRM extension community

On the vtiger team's website, `vtiger.com`, at the time of the writing of this book, if you click on the **Extensions** tab, you'll find their extension marketplace. It is organized into several categories such as **Featured**, **Top Rated**, and **Most Recent**. You can also browse the extensions by the version of vtiger that were designed for:

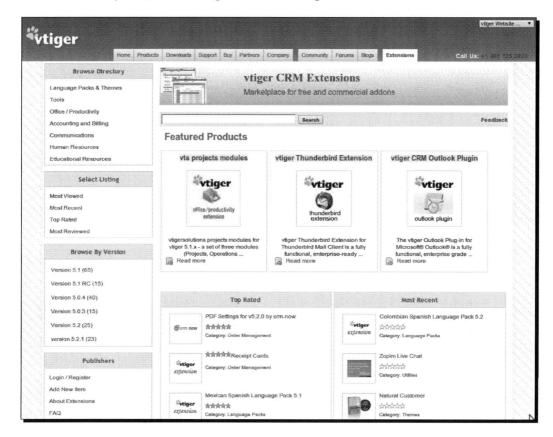

In the vtiger CRM Extensions Marketplace you'll find over 100 add-ons that allow you to customize the PDFs in vtiger as well as Windows plugins like the Outlook Plugin. Contributors to the extensions marketplace include vtiger solutions partners, hosting partners, independent developers, and the vtiger team themselves.

Some of the extensions will have a fee. You do have to be careful in selecting the right extension. You should make sure that the extension has good reviews. You should also try to Google the extension and try to find any related discussions on forums or blog sites. For example, beyond the version that is produced by the vtiger CRM team, there are several versions of the Outlook plugin. Some are written for specific versions of Outlook or Windows.

Installing extensions

Many of the extensions require you to download a compressed file and unzip it into your vtiger installation directory. However, since version 5.1, a Module Manager is now included. Any extensions written specifically for Module Manager are very easy to install. You simply upload the compressed file to your vtiger instance and Module Manager takes care of the rest.

Even though its not quite there yet, vtiger CRM is slowly moving towards a paradigm that caters more to the end user. The vtiger team is a group made up mostly of technical people—developers. However, the addition of Module Manager is clear proof that the vtiger community is making their voice heard and also helping to fulfill their own requirements.

Let's roll up our sleeves now and try out an extension.

Time for action – downloading and installing a vtiger extension

One very useful vtiger extension is the **Daily Activity Report Tool (DART)**. The DART helps a sales manager keep an eye on day-to-day performance and keep everyone on the team productive.

In this exercise, we're going to install this module:

1. First, go to vtiger.com and click on the Extension Marketplace:

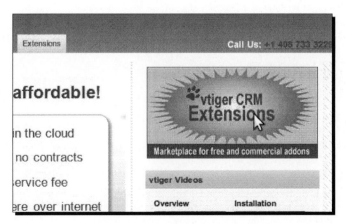

2. Now search for **daily activity**.

3. Click on **Daily Activity Report Tool for vtiger CRM**:

4. Click on **Download**:

5. Download the zip file to your desktop.

6. Since the Daily Activity Report Tool uses the Module Manager, it will be an easy installation. Log in to your vtiger instance.

7. Click on **Settings | Module Manager**:

8. Click on **Custom Modules**:

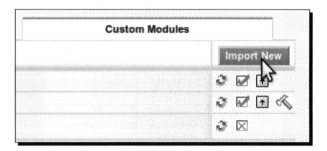

9. Click on **Choose File**:

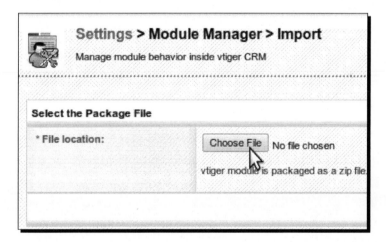

10. Browse to and select the file you downloaded to your desktop. It should be named something like **DART-1.1.zip**.

11. Click on **Import**:

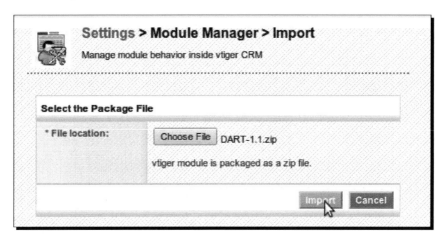

12. You'll be shown the module details so you can verify them. Accept the license agreement and click **Yes** to proceed with the module installation:

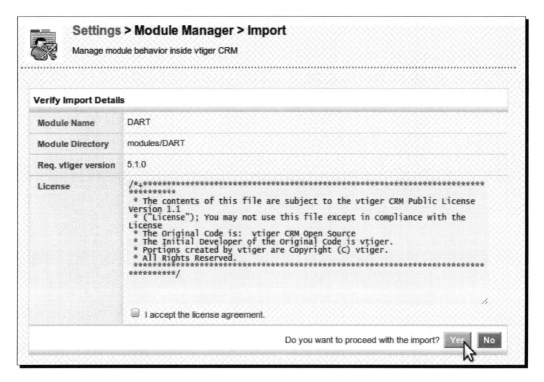

13. You'll be shown the details of the module installation process. Click **Finish** to complete:

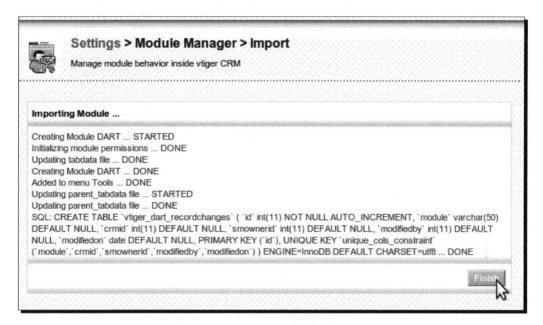

14. Now in the **Tools** menu, you can see the new module:

What just happened?

We successfully downloaded DART, a community extension, from the vtiger CRM Extensions Marketplace and installed it using the Module Manager.

Now open the DART tool by going to **Tools | DART**. This tool will show you a summary of activities for all users that take place in vtiger CRM. You'll be able to see what calls have been made, new business that has been won, and new relationships that have been formed:

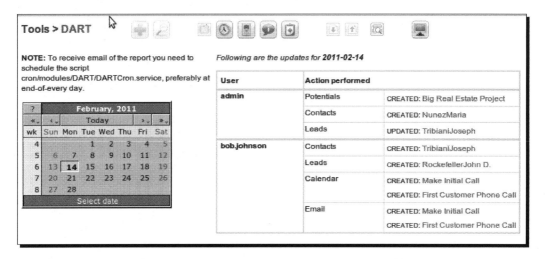

Have a go hero

DART also features a daily email that includes an activity report. Try to set up the daily email status report. You'll have to set up a cron job or a Scheduled Task in order to do this. You can refer to the section *How to create a workflow in vtiger CRM* in Chapter 6 to see how to set up a cron job or Scheduled Task.

Some useful vtiger CRM extensions

There are many other useful vtiger CRM extensions. Here are just a few of the most popular ones.

Language packs

vtiger CRM is currently translated into over 12 different languages. Check the marketplace to see which ones are supported.

vtiger CRM outlook plugin

If your organization relies heavily on Exchange Server and/or Microsoft Outlook for email and collaboration, you can easily integrate vtiger. Just install this plugin and you'll have a vtiger toolbar inside of Outlook that will allow you to record emails, calendar events, and make notes all within Outlook.

Notice that, within Outlook, you can select emails to be sent to vtiger:

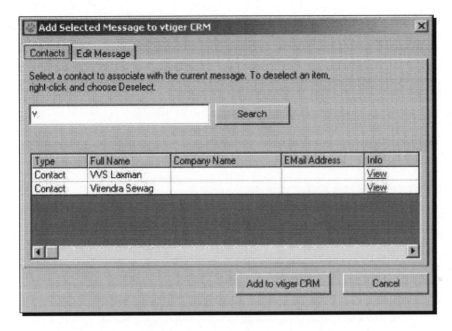

Also, when you synchronize, you'll have full control over what is synchronized and how, meaning which version will win if there is a conflict:

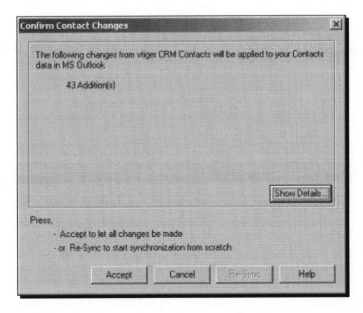

Here's a full list of all of the features of the Outlook plugin. You'll be able to:

◆ Synchronize contacts between Outlook and vtiger CRM

◆ Apply filters to emails in Outlook to add specific emails to vtiger

◆ Synchronize your calendar (calls and meeting appointments) between Outlook and vtiger

◆ Add incoming and outgoing emails from Outlook to specific contacts in vtiger CRM

◆ Synchronize tasks between Outlook and vtiger

◆ Manage and resolve synchronization conflicts between Outlook and vtiger CRM

Vtiger Thunderbird extension

If you use the open source email client, Thunderbird, you can add outgoing or incoming email messages to vtiger CRM records and synchronize contacts. Notice that it provides a handy, useful toolbar for synchronizing data between Thunderbird and vtiger:

First, as in the Outlook plugin, you must configure the plugin with your instance of vtiger. You just enter your instance URL, username, and Access Key, which you can access from **My Preferences** link at the top of the vtiger interface:

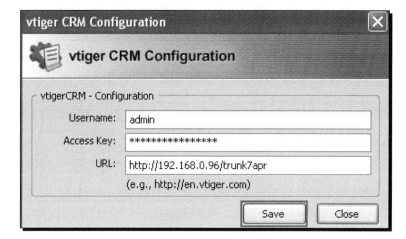

Then you can easily add messages to vtiger from within Mozilla Thunderbird:

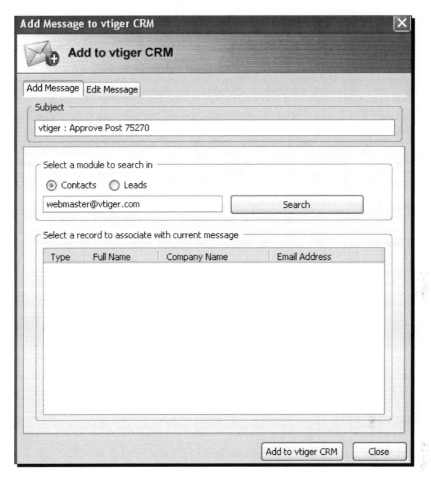

PDF Configurator and settings

You can't really do much in the way of customizations to the PDF forms in vtiger out-of-the-box. However, a community member created a module called PDF Configurator that gives you far more control over the look and feel of PDF forms that you may send to your customers and prospects. There are a few extensions like this on the marketplace that allow you to significantly improve the out-of-the-box PDF documents in vtiger CRM like invoices and quotes. It allows you to get a better looking logo and add all kinds of custom fields.

Here is a sample of what the PDF Configurator can produce:

BitConstructor Co., Ltd Tel./Fax.: +66 2 168 40 50
48/1 Soi Sukhumvit 11, Email: office@bitconstructor.com
Klongtoey Nua, Wattana Web: http://www.bitconstructor.com
Bangkok, Thailand 10110

Invoice No	INV1		**Customer No**	ACC5
			Customer	Sample Company

Billing Address
Sample Company
Sesame Str. 25
CH-8048 Geneva
Switzerland

Our Contact	Tibor Sekelj	**Issue Date**	25.11.2009
Your Contact	Max Seifert	**Due Date**	25.11.2009

INVOICE

Product Code	Product Name	Qty	Price	Total
PRO6	Custom Programming	1.0	630.00	630.00
PRO7	Graphic Services	2.0	30.00	60.00
Net Total				690.00
Tax (7 %)				48.30
Grand Total (in CHF)				**738.30**

Description

Changes on vTiger

- Chinese currency

- PDF modifications

- EP-VP comparison report

- Task notifications

We hope you are happy with our service and thank you kindly for working with us.

If we can be of any further assistance, please let us know.

Warm regards

BitConstructor Co., Ltd.

Bank: Siam Commercial Bank PCL Account Number: 040-304026-9
Branch: Chaiyod Account Name: BitConstructor Co. Ltd
Swift Code: SICOTHBKXXX Income Tax Number: 3031940697   Page 1

You can see how much of an improvement it is from the out-of-the-box PDF forms:

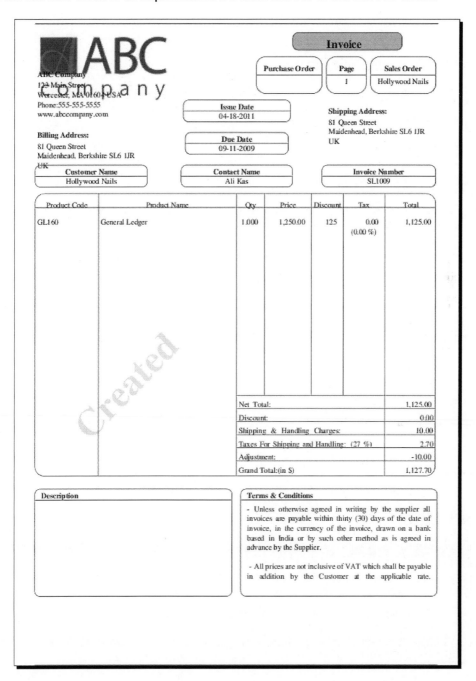

JoomTiger

JoomTiger allows you to integrate certain vtiger CRM features with your Joomla-based website, like inserting leads into vtiger from your website. Specifically, you can:

◆ Capture leads from your Joomla-based website into vtiger with a custom form on your website.

◆ Easily validate the data that users enter into the lead form.

◆ User Captcha security in form submission. The user will have to enter characters that they see generated in an image to verify their legitimate input.

Drupal module for vtiger webforms

This is similar to JoomTiger but allows you to integrate vtiger webforms into your Drupal-based website. If you're familiar with Drupal, you can see here that this module installs into Drupal as a normal Drupal module:

Summary

In this chapter we learned about vtiger CRM extensions, where to get them, and how to install them:

◆ We checked out the vtiger CRM Extension Marketplace

◆ We downloaded and installed a vtiger CRM community extension

We covered the concept of using extensions to customize vtiger for your organization. In the next chapter, we'll take this a step further as we explore theming in vtiger CRM.

8
Facing the Tiger—vtiger Theming

Most organizations have a brand that they want to promote internally as well as externally. While they may be open to adopting open source software, they will most likely want the solution to fit in with their established brand. Theming in vtiger CRM makes this not just possible, but fairly easy.

In this chapter we'll discuss:

◆ vtiger CRM theme elements

◆ How to customize the lead detail interface

◆ How to create a custom theme

 This chapter assumes that you understand and/or have experience with HTML and CSS. For a more in-depth discussion of HTML and CSS, please check out Packt titles on this subject.

vtiger CRM theme elements

vtiger CRM uses some pretty standard user interface elements such as menu bars, side bars, tabs, and buttons. Although you do need to know HTML and CSS to change the appearance of these elements, the good news is that you don't need to know vtiger CRM's template engine, Smarty, to make your desired changes.

Taking a peak behind the scenes

Let's check out the CSS that controls these style elements. To do this, navigate to the root of your vtiger CRM installation and find the themes folder. You'll remember your vtiger root directory after having installed vtiger in Chapter 2. In themes folder, open the folder called `softed`. This is the default theme in vtiger CRM. In the `softed` folder, you'll find a file named the standard `style.css`. Here's the exact location from your root:

`vtigercrm/themes/softed/style.css`

This file controls the majority of the styles in vtiger CRM, with the exception of vtiger's Webmail client and chat feature. It's fairly well commented, so you should be able to find your way around pretty easily. However, the best way to find out which piece of CSS code controls which UI element is to use a neat feature of the Google Chrome web browser. It's called **Inspect Element**.

Navigate to the page of the UI element you'd like to modify. Now, right-click on that element and then click on **Inspect Element**:

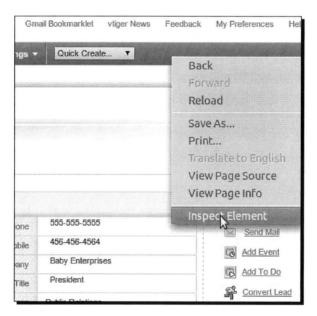

After you click on **Inspect Element**, the inspector window will pop up and you'll see the HTML code and CSS for the menu bar:

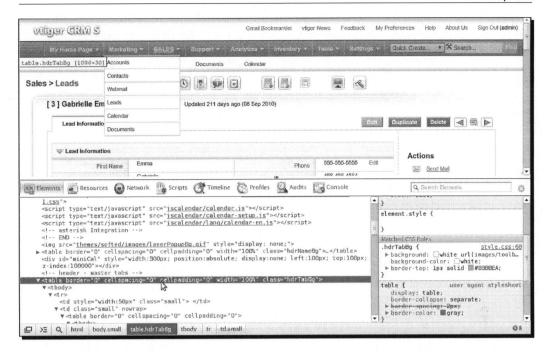

When the HTML code pops up at the bottom left, you can navigate the HTML hierarchy to find the specific element you're looking for. Here, we have found that the menu bar is an HTML table and it has a style class called `hdrTabBg`. In the bottom-right pane, we can see the styles applied to that CSS class. You can now change those values and see them update in the browser.

Once you've made the changes you like, you can copy and paste them into the `style.css` file.

This is a quick and dirty way to get the style changes you want. The best way to do it is by creating your own custom theme. In the next section, we'll create a custom theme and change a few elements together. This should set you off on a course to finish the theme on your own.

How to create a custom theme

Let's navigate back to the themes folder:

`vtigercrm/themes`

In there, you'll see several folders—one for each of the themes that you see in the **Theme** dropdown on the vtiger CRM login page. Log in to vtiger with each of the themes and see which one you like best. We're going to copy it and use it as a starting point.

Time for action – creating a custom theme

Our goal in this exercise will be to make the primary menu options appear as tabs instead of a menu bar that goes all the way across the screen. We're going to copy the folder of the theme you like most and we're going to add our own company logo and modify the `style.css` file. You can go as far as modifying the images that are referenced by the CSS file, but for the purposes of this exercise, we're going to stick to the logo and the CSS code:

1. Copy the folder of the theme you like. For this exercise, I'm copying the theme called **softed**.

2. Paste it into the **themes** folder and rename it as **custom**.

3. Now log out of vtiger CRM if you're logged in and log in again.

4. You should now see your new theme listed in the **Theme** dropdown:

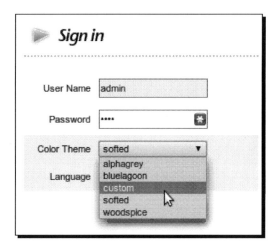

5. Now to make our theme "custom" let's change something. Let's change the logo.

6. Let's take our company logo and put it into an area about 170 x 50 pixels and let's leave a bit of space at the top and to the left so it looks right. While you'll use your company logo, I'll use mine:

7. Save your new logo with the file name `vtiger-crm.gif`.

8. Place this logo file into the `images` folder inside your `custom` folder. Here's the full path of the images folder where you want to put your logo: `vtigercrm/themes/custom/images`.

9. Now let's change the color of the secondary menu bar to match our company colors. Let's go to the `style.css` file and find the class called `level2Bg`.

10. I'm going to remove the background image and change the color value of the background to blue that matches my company colors. I'm also changing the top and bottom border colors. Finally, I'm increasing the font size of the menu elements to make them more easily readable. The code looks like the following. The changed lines are highlighted. You can make changes based on your company colors:

```css
.level2Bg {
    background-color: #2D92CA;
    font-family: Arial, Helvetica, sans-serif;
    font-size: 14px;
    border-top: 1px solid #2D92CA;
    border-bottom: 1px solid #BFBFBF;
    color: white;
}
```

11. To create the appearance of tabs in the main menu elements, let's change the background of the `hdrTabBg` bar that we looked at in our earlier example to white. Here's the before and after code. We're essentially removing all styles from this class. Remove the properties `background`, `background-color`, and `border-top`:

```css
.hdrTabBg {
}
```

12. Now we're going to create the tabs themselves. First we'll set the color for the unselected tabs to blend in with the secondary menu bar. Let's find the class called `tabUnSelected` and modify it. Remove the background property altogether. Then we're just going to modify the `font-size` as highlighted below:

```css
.tabUnSelected {
    background-color: #A7CE38;
    background: #fff url(images/toolbar-bg.png) bottom repeat-x;
    font-family: Arial, Helvetica, sans-serif;
    font-size: 10px;
    padding-left: 10px;
    padding-right: 10px;
    padding-top: 2px;
```

```
      padding-bottom: 2px;
      border-bottom: 0px solid white;
   }
```

13. We're also going to increase the font size of the menu links. Let's modify the classes `tabSelected a` and `tabUnselected a`. We're going to increase the font sizes according to the code below:

```
.tabSelected a {
   color: white;
   text-transform: uppercase;
   text-decoration: underline;
   font-size: 14px;
}
.tabUnSelected a {
   font-family: Arial, Helvetica, sans-serif;
   font-size: 14px;
   color: white;
   font-weight: bold;
}
```

14. Let's set the color of the selected tab to stand out. Let's once again remove the `background` **property and just leave the** `background-color`:

```
.tabSelected {
   background-color: #2D92CA;
   font-family: Arial, Helvetica, sans-serif;
   font-weight: bold;
   font-size: 10px;
   padding-left: 10px;
   padding-right: 10px;
   padding-top: 2px;
   padding-bottom: 2px;
   border-bottom: 0px solid white;
}
```

15. Finally, let's make the color of the links in the secondary menu bar white, so they stand out better. We'll change the color property of the `level2bg` class:

```
   .level2Bg a {
color: white;
   }
```

What just happened?

We copied the default theme in vtiger and customized it. We replaced the vtiger logo with our company logo. We also changed the menu bar to look like tabs that match our company colors.

Pop quiz – Creating a custom theme

Let's test our skills with vtiger theming so far.

1. Where can you find vtiger's themes?

   a. vtiger.com

   b. c:\themes

   c. The themes folder in vtiger's root (vtigercrm/themes)

2. What is the best way to find out what the CSS code is for a particular vtiger screen element?

   a. By searching on Google

   b. Using Google Chrome's element inspector

   c. Scrolling through vtiger's `style.css` file until you find it

3. What file do you have to replace to change the logo displayed in the theme?

   a. `c:\vtiger-logo.jpg`

   b. `vtigercrm/themes/[THEME NAME]/images/vtiger-crm.gif`

   c. `c:\Program Files\vtiger\logo.jpg`

Have a go hero – Make it your own

So, in the previous exercise, we used aimtheory company colors for the menu tabs. Now you can really delve in and experiment with the CSS. If this is your first exposure to CSS, by all means, take this opportunity to play around and get familiar with it.

Give the following a try and then keep going with it:

◆ Modify the CSS to use your company's colors for the menu tabs.

◆ Try to apply some new CSS3 effects like text shadow and rounded corners. (See Packt titles for more on CSS3).

◆ Take the tabs a step further and change the actual drop down menus to match the tab colors and font size.

Customizing the lead detail interface

So, by copying a theme, we've made some minor changes and we now have our own "custom" theme that we can choose as we log in to vtiger. Now, using similar CSS techniques, we can make our theme truly custom and change the look and feel of other parts of the vtiger CRM UI. Let's try something else. Now we're going to customize the interface on the **Lead Detail** screen.

You should note that the techniques in the following section will also modify the interfaces of the other details screens as well as—accounts, contacts, opportunities—any CRM entity in the system. This way your changes will be universal and uniform.

Time for action – changing the look and feel of the lead detail page

Let's navigate to the lead detail page by going to **Sales | Leads**. Then click on a lead to get to the detail page. You can use Google Chrome's element inspector once again to examine the code behind the screen elements. We'll make the changes in `style.css` once again:

1. Let's make the lead name/title nice and big. Let's change the font-size property to 18 pixel instead of 14 pixel:

```
.dvHeaderText {
  font-family: Arial, Helvetica, sans-serif;
  font-size: 18px;
  color: black;
  font-weight: bold;
}
```

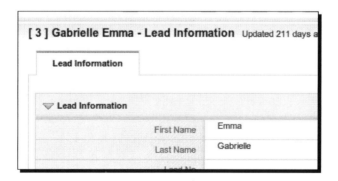

2. Now the lead name is larger and more readable:

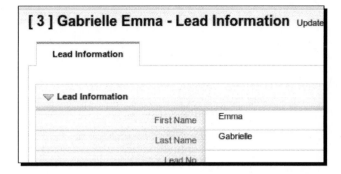

3. Let's remove the unnecessary background image for a cleaner look. Just remove the background property altogether:

```
.showPanelBg {
}
```

From:

To:

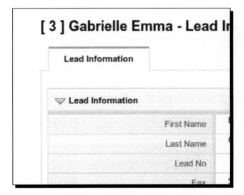

4. Now let's increase the font size of the detail text so it's a bit easier to read. To do that, we're going to modify the `small` class in the `style.css` file. Someone's idea of "small" is a little too small for my taste:

```
.small {
  font-family: Arial, Helvetica, sans-serif;
  font-size: 14px;
  color: black;
}
```

From:

First Name	Emma
Last Name	Gabrielle
Lead No	
Fax	456-456-4564
Email	emma.gabrielle@babyenterprises.com
Website	
Lead Status	Contacted
Rating	Acquired

To:

ation	
First Name	Emma
Last Name	Gabrielle
Lead No	
Fax	456-456-4564
Email	emma.gabrielle@babyenterprises.com
Website	
Lead Status	Contacted
Rating	Acquired

What just happened?

We changed the look and feel of the lead detail page as well as the detail pages for the other CRM entities in the system—accounts, contacts, opportunities, products, and so on.

The lead detail page in the default theme of vtiger CRM has font sizes that are a bit too small, so we increased the font sizes and we also made the page look a bit cleaner by removing some unnecessary background images.

Have a go hero – Keep changing the CSS

Now that you've gotten your feet wet with vtiger's `style.css` file and Google Chrome's code inspector tool, try to venture further and make some customizations based on your own preferences. For instance, you could:

◆ Change the font size in other parts of the interface

◆ Change the font family to something other than the Arial-based font in vtiger

◆ Change or add more color into the interface

◆ Add your own custom graphics in the background, as section headers or as bullets

◆ Add CSS effects for a more pleasing look

◆ If your company has a style guide, you can begin to incorporate those style elements into your own branded vtiger interface

Summary

In this chapter we learned how to create a custom theme using vtiger's `style.css` file:

◆ We created our theme called "custom" by copying the vtiger CRM default theme

◆ We then customized the theme by:
  ❑ Replacing the logo file
  ❑ Changing the main menu bar to appear as tabs
  ❑ Increasing font sizes
  ❑ Removing unnecessary background images

By creating our own custom theme, we have not only gotten the colors and styles that we want, but we have also increased readability by increasing font sizes. Keep experimenting with the CSS and making changes according to your organization's preference.

In the next chapter, we'll learn how we can integrate vtiger with external systems.

9

Kitty, Play Nice!—Integrating vtiger

Any organization that is prone to adopt an open source software package is bound to be using another—or soon will be. In this chapter, you will learn how to do some basic integration between vtiger and external systems such as your company website.

In this chapter we'll discuss:

◆ vtiger's API

◆ How to use vtiger's web lead feature

◆ How to include custom fields in the lead form

To go through the exercises in this chapter, you'll need basic knowledge of HTML. If you already understand basic web development concepts, then you'll also be well prepared to delve into vtiger CRM's API.

The vtiger CRM API

For you developers out there, all of the ins and outs of vtiger CRM's API are fully documented at `http://api.vtiger.com`. For those of you not familiar with API's, API stands for **Application Programming Interface**. It's an interface for computers rather than humans.

What does the API do?

To illustrate—you can access the human interface of vtiger CRM by logging in with your username and password. The screens that are shown to you with all of the buttons and links make up the human interface. An API, on the other hand, is an interface for other computers. Computers don't need the fancy stuff that we humans do in the interface—it's all text.

What is the benefit of the API?

With an API, vtiger allows other computer systems to inform it and also ask it questions. This makes everyone's life easier, especially if it means you don't have to type the same data twice into two systems.

Here's an example. You have a website where people make sales inquiries and you capture that information as a sales lead. You might receive that information as an email. At that point you could just leave the data in your email and refer to it as needed (which many people still do) or you could enter it into a CRM tool like vtiger so you can keep track of your leads.

You can take it one step further by using vtiger's API. You can tell your website how to talk to vtiger's API and now your website can send the leads directly into vtiger, and...Voila! When you log in, the person who just made an inquiry on your website is now a lead in vtiger.

Sending a lead into vtiger CRM from your website

Well, what are we waiting for?! Let's give it a try. There is a plugin/extension in vtiger called **Webforms** and it uses the vtiger API to get data into vtiger. In the following exercises, we're going to:

◆ Configure the Webforms plugin

◆ Create a webform on your company website

IMPORTANT NOTE: If you want to be able to send leads into vtiger from your website, your vtiger installation must be accessible on the Internet. If you have installed vtiger on a computer or server on your internal network, then you won't be able to send leads into vtiger from your website, because your website won't be able to connect with the computer/server that vtiger is running on.

Time for action – configuring the Webforms plugin

OK, let's roll up our sleeves and get ready to do a little code editing. Let's take a look first:

1. Let's navigate to the Webforms configuration file in `vtigercrm/modules/Webforms/Webforms.config.php`

2. Let's open it up with a text editor like Notepad. Here's what it might look like by default:

```php
<?php
/*+*****************************************************************
*******************
 * The contents of this file are subject to the vtiger CRM Public
License Version 1.0
 * ("License"); You may not use this file except in compliance
with the License
 * The Original Code is:  vtiger CRM Open Source
 * The Initial Developer of the Original Code is vtiger.
 * Portions created by vtiger are Copyright (C) vtiger.
 * All Rights Reserved.
 *****************************************************************
*******************/

$enableAppKeyValidation = true;
$defaultUserName = 'admin';
$defaultUserAccessKey = 'iFOdqrI81S5UhNTa';

$defaultOwner = 'admin';
$successURL = '';
$failureURL = '';

/**
 * JSON or HTML. if incase success and failure URL is NOT
specified.
 */
$defaultSuccessAction = 'HTML';

$defaultSuccessMessage = 'LBL_SUCCESS';

?>
```

3. We have to be concerned with several lines here. Specifically, they're the ones that contain the following:

- ❑ `$defaultUserName`: This will most likely be the admin user, although it can be any user that you create in your vtiger CRM system.

- ❑ `$defaultUserAccessKey`: This key is used for authentication when your website will access vtiger's API. You can access this key by logging in to vtiger and clicking on the **My Preferences** link at the top right. It needs to be the key for the username assigned to the `$defaultUserName` variable.

❑ `$defaultOwner`: This user will be assigned all of the new leads created by this form by default.

❑ `$successURL`: If the lead submission is successful, this is the URL to which you want to send the user after they entered their information. This would typically be a web page that would thank the user for their submission and provide any additional sales information.

❑ `$failureURL`: This is the URL which you want to send the user if the submission fails. This would typically be a web page that would say something like, "We apologize, but something has gone wrong. Please try again".

4. Now you'll need to fill in the values with the information from our own installation of vtiger CRM.

5. Save the `Webforms.config.php` and close it. We've finished completing the configuration of the Webforms module.

What just happened?

We configured the Webforms module in vtiger CRM. We modified the Webform plugin's configuration file, `Webforms.config.php`. Now the Webforms module will:

◆ Be able to authenticate lead submissions that come from your website

◆ Assign all new leads to the admin user by default (you'll be able to change this)

◆ Send the user to a thank you page, should the lead submission into vtiger succeed

◆ Send the user to an "Oops" page, should the lead submission into vtiger fail

How to set up a webform on your website

Now that we have everything configured on the vtiger side of things, let's make some simples changes on your website that will allow you to send a lead from your website directly into vtiger.

Time for action – setting up a lead form on your website

Here is where some basic knowledge of HTML will come into play:

1. You'll need a page on your website that will "host" the webform. Open up that web page with your HTML editor.

2. Now, in the body of the web page, (in between the `<body>` and `</body>` tags) create a form using the HTML code below. Where you can see VTIGER-URL you need to put it in the URL of your vtiger installation:

```
<form method="POST" action="http://[VTIGER-URL]/modules/Webforms/
post.php">
    <input type="hidden" value="Leads" name="moduleName" />
    <table>
        <tbody>
            <tr>
                <td><label>Last Name</label></td>
                <td><input type="text" name="lastname" value="" />
                </td>
            </tr>
            <tr>
                <td><label>First Name</td>
                <td><input type="text" name="firstname" value="" />
                </td>
            </tr>
            <tr>
                <td><label>Company</td>
                <td><input type="text" name="company" value="" /></td>
            </tr>
        </tbody>
    <table>
    <input type="submit" value="Submit" />
</form>
```

3. Now save your web page.

4. Now go to the URL of the web page that you just added the webform to.

5. Fill out all of the fields. Note that if the fields are required in vtiger and they are not all completed, the lead submission will fail.

6. Submit the form.

7. Log in to vtiger and go to **Sales | Leads**.

8. You should see the new lead in your list of leads.

What just happened?

We used the vtiger CRM API to get data from an external system into your installation of vtiger. We used the Webform component of vtiger to create a form on your company website. Now when visitors to your website make a sales inquiry, that data will go straight into vtiger.

How to use custom fields in a webform

Now suppose that you have customized your Leads module and you have 20 or 30 custom fields. You may have very specific information that you want to capture in that first step so that the next step in the sales process can be more successful and move the lead closer to a potential sale.

In this case, you'll need to modify the plain webform from the example above and include form fields that will connect with your custom fields once the lead hits vtiger. Let's try it.

Time for Action – using custom fields in a webform

1. Once again, you'll need a page on your website that will "host" the webform. Open up that web page with your HTML editor.

2. Now, in the body of the web page, (in between the `<body>` and `</body>` tags) create a form using the HTML code below. Where you can see VTIGER-URL you need to put it in the URL of your vtiger installation:

```
<form method="POST" action="http://[VTIGER-URL]/modules/Webforms/
post.php">
    <input type="hidden" value="Leads" name="moduleName" />
    <table>
        <tbody>
            <tr>
                <td><label>Last Name</label></td>
                <td><input type="text" name="lastname" value="" />
                </td>
            </tr>
            <tr>
                <td><label>First Name</td>
                <td><input type="text" name="firstname" value="" />
                </td>
            </tr>
            <tr>
                <td><label>Company</td>
```

```
            <td><input type="text" name="company" value="" /></td>
        </tr>
      </tbody>
    <table>
    <input type="submit" value="Submit" />
</form>
```

3. Here's where we'll add the custom field. We have to create a new HTML input element and name it to match the name that our custom field has in the database.

4. First, we have to find out what the field name is in the database. To do this execute the following on your MySQL server:

```
use database vtigercrm;

SELECT fieldname FROM vtiger_field WHERE fieldlabel LIKE "Custom
Text Field" AND tablename = "vtiger_leadscf";
```

5. Note that you'll have to modify a couple of things:

   ❏ You'll have to substitute `vtigercrm` in the statement `use database vtigercrm;` with the name of your vtiger database

   ❏ You'll have to substitute `"Custom Text Field"` in the following `SELECT` statement with the label of your custom field

6. MySQL will return the field name that you'll use in your webform. That is the value that you'll need to use on your webform. In this example that value is **cf_476**.

7. Now edit your web page to look like the following:

```
<form method="POST" action="http://[VTIGER-URL]/modules/Webforms/
post.php">
    <input type="hidden" value="Leads" name="moduleName" />
    <table>
      <tbody>
        <tr>
            <td><label>Last Name</label></td>
            <td><input type="text" name="lastname" value="" />
            </td>
        </tr>
        <tr>
            <td><label>First Name</td>
            <td><input type="text" name="firstname" value="" />
            </td>
        </tr>
        <tr>
            <td><label>Company</td>
            <td><input type="text" name="company" value="" /></td>
```

```
            </tr>
            <tr>
               <td><label>Custom Text</td>
               <td><input type="text" name="cf_476" value="" /></td>
            </tr>
         </tbody>
      <table>
      <input type="submit" value="Submit" />
   </form>
```

8. Now save your web page.

9. Now go to the URL of the web page that you just added the webform to.

10. Fill out all of the fields. Note that if the fields are required in vtiger and they are not all completed, the lead submission will fail.

11. Submit the form.

12. Log in to vtiger and go to **Sales | Leads**.

13. You should see the new lead in your list of leads with your custom field, **Custom Text Field**, populated.

What just happened?

We created a form from HTML and inserted it onto a web page of your company website. We looked through vtiger CRM's MySQL database and found the database name of your custom field. We then used the database name of your custom field in the webform. Now you can add as many custom forms as you would like to your webform.

Summary

In this chapter, we learned that vtiger has the power to integrate with external systems. In particular:

- vtiger CRM's API is an interface to external systems
- The Webforms module in vtiger is a powerful tool that you can use to eliminate the need for double-entry of data
- We were able to create a "portal" on your company website where prospective customers can make a sales inquiry and directly insert that inquiry into your installation of vtiger CRM for followup

In the next chapter, we'll take the concept of custom to the next level with **custom modules**.

10
From Cub to King—Growing with vtiger

We've all heard the horror stories of when a performing animal turns on its trainer. After years of great companionship, something went wrong. Many organizations that adopt vtiger are startups. As your organization grows, so will its needs. How will you keep vtiger in a place where it will continue to enhance your organization's effectiveness? How will you implement your organization's changes into vtiger? Could vtiger change too much and effectively turn on your organization? In this chapter, we'll consider how to customize vtiger and use best practices to manage a vtiger implementation over the long term.

In this chapter we shall:

◆ Create a custom module

◆ Integrate a custom module with vtiger core modules

◆ Discuss best practices on how to manage your vtiger code over the long term

◆ Discuss how to use the cloud to support vtiger

So let's get on with it...

Important preliminary points

As we create a custom module in this chapter, we'll be dealing with PHP code and MySQL code as well. It will also be helpful to:

◆ Download and review the sample Payslip module source code: `http://forge.vtiger.com/frs/download.php/753/Payslip-5.1.0-source.zip`.

◆ Download and review the vtlib documentation: `https://docs.google.com/viewer?url=http://forge.vtiger.com/frs/download.php/678/vtlib-2.1.pdf`.

What is vtlib?

vtlib is a library of PHP code that the vtiger team created that simplifies the custom module creation process. Prior to vtlib, creating a vtiger custom module was arduous. It required that you had to copy of different PHP and template files and modify each of them individually. vtlib does all of the modifications for you.

For more information about vtlib, check out the `vtiger.com` website:

`wiki.vtiger.com/index.php/vtiger520:Vtlib`

Creating a custom module

 It is difficult to "undo" the changes that vtlib makes. So it's advisable that you do your work with vtlib on a copy of your production system. Alternatively, you can backup your production code and then rely on that for any needed rollbacks.

Creating a custom module will allow you to manage more aspects of your organization than vtiger is ready for out-of-the-box. For example, if your customers have multiple locations and there are multiple contacts at those multiple locations, then vtiger's default configuration won't work.

You would need to add an entity module that would manage "Locations". Each location would be linked to a customer account and to, potentially, multiple contacts.

Before we get into things, please briefly review the code in the sample payslip module. You'll be able to copy most of the code for a simple entity module, even with relationships.

The basic process is:

◆ Create a PHP script that will create the module

◆ Put the PHP script into your vtiger root directory

◆ Execute the PHP script. It will utilize the vtlib code in vtiger and make all of the necessary changes

Once the script has finished, you have to make a few more simple changes to file names and contents.

Before we get started, let's make sure to enable logging in vtiger just in case something goes wrong while we're creating our custom module.

Time for action – setting up debugging

1. Open up the file `config.performance.php` in the root of your vtiger directory (named `vtigercrm` by default) and find the following line:

   ```
   'LOG4PHP_DEBUG' => false,
   ```

   Change it to:

   ```
   'LOG4PHP_DEBUG' => true,
   ```

2. Now, open up the file `log4php.properties` also in the root of your vtiger directory and change:

   ```
   log4php.rootLogger=FATAL,A1
   ```

   Change it to the following:

   ```
   log4php.rootLogger=DEBUG,A1
   ```

3. Now, to see what's happening with vtiger, you can check the file `vtigercrm.log` in the `logs` folder of your vtiger root directory.

4. If you're running on Linux, you can use the following command to get a live view of the log in a terminal window:

   ```
   ianrossi@ianrossi-laptop:/var/www/vtigercrm~$ tail -f logs/
   vtigercrm.log
   ```

5. Make sure to execute this from your vtiger root directory.

6. There is no tail equivalent in Windows, so you'll just have to keep refreshing the `vtigercrm.log` file.

What just happened?

We just set up debugging in vtiger so we can know what's going on behind the scenes as we modify and test our enhancements.

Now let's dig in and create our custom module script.

Time for action – creating a custom module in vtiger

So, if you wanted to create this "Locations" module that would track your customer's different locations, you would create a PHP script with the following sections:

1. Let's start by creating the PHP file properly and including some nice neat HTML supplied by the vtiger team. This code is creating the HTML header, defining the CSS for the theme and displaying the vtiger logo:

```php
<?php
// Just a bit of HTML formatting
echo '<!DOCTYPE html PUBLIC "-//W3C//DTD HTML 4.01 Transitional//
EN" "http://www.w3.org/TR/html4/loose.dtd">';
echo '<html><head><title>vtlib Module Script</title>';
echo '<style type="text/css">@import url("themes/softed/style.
css");br { display: block; margin: 2px; }</style>';
echo '</head><body class=small style="font-size: 12px; margin:
2px; padding: 2px;">';
echo '<a href="index.php"><img src="themes/softed/images/vtiger-
crm.gif" alt="vtiger CRM" title="vtiger CRM" border=0></a><hr
style="height: 1px">';
```

2. Start by turning on debugging and including necessary PHP files:

```php
$Vtiger_Utils_Log = true;

include_once('vtlib/Vtiger/Menu.php');
include_once('vtlib/Vtiger/Module.php');
```

3. Then create your module instance and save it. Finally, the call to `initWebservice()` will initialize the webservice setup for our new module instance:

```php
$module = new Vtiger_Module();
$module->name = 'Location';
$module->save();
$module->initWebservice();
```

4. Now initialize, or create, the tables required for your new module:

```
$module->initTables();
```

5. Now add the module to the menu system. We're going to add it to the Sales dropdown menu in the main menu bar:

```
$menu = Vtiger_Menu::getInstance('Sales');
$menu->addModule($module);
```

6. Now add a block for the basic module information:

```
$block1 = new Vtiger_Block();
$block1->label = 'LBL_LOCATION_INFORMATION';
$module->addBlock($block1);
```

7. Now add a block for custom fields, so you can extend it in the future through the user interface:

```
$block2 = new Vtiger_Block();
$block2->label = 'LBL_CUSTOM_INFORMATION';
$module->addBlock($block2);
```

8. Now let's create the fields for the module. First we'll create the Location Name field.

`$field1->table = $module->basetable;` indicates that the field will reside in the base table of your new custom module.

`$field1->uitype = 2;` means a required text box. See here for more UI types: `http://wiki.vtiger.com/index.php/Ui_types`

`$field1->typeofdata = 'V~M';` indicates that the field is Varchar and is Mandatory. See here for more data types: http://wiki. vtiger.com/index.php/INV...~ON

```
$field1 = new Vtiger_Field();
$field1->name = 'locationname';
$field1->label = 'Location Name';
$field1->table = $module->basetable;
$field1->column = 'locationname';
$field1->columntype = 'VARCHAR(255)';
$field1->uitype = 2;
$field1->typeofdata = 'V~M';
$block1->addField($field1);
```

9. Set the name field as the field identifier:

```
$module->setEntityIdentifier($field1);
```

10. Now add the **Location Address** field:

```
$field2 = new Vtiger_Field();
$field2->name = 'locationaddress';
$field2->label = 'Location Address';
$field2->table = $module->basetable;
$field2->column = 'locationaddress';
$field2->columntype = 'VARCHAR(255)';
$field2->uitype = 2;
$field2->typeofdata = 'V~O';// Varchar~Optional
$block1->addField($field2); /** table and column are automatically
set */
```

11. Now add the **Location Address 2** field:

```
//Location address 2 field
$field3 = new Vtiger_Field();
$field3->name = 'locationaddress2';
$field3->label = 'Location Address 2';
$field3->table = $module->basetable;
$field3->column = 'locationaddress2';
$field3->columntype = 'VARCHAR(255)';
$field3->uitype = 2;
$field3->typeofdata = 'V~O'; // Date~Mandatory
$block1->addField($field3);
```

12. Now add the **Location City** field:

```
$field4 = new Vtiger_Field();
$field4->name = 'locationcity';
$field4->label= 'Location City';
$field4->table = $module->basetable;
$field4->column = 'locationcity';
$field4->columntype = 'VARCHAR(255)';
$field4->uitype = 2;
$field4->typeofdata = 'V~O';
$block1->addField($field4);
```

13. Now add the **Location State** field:

```
$field5 = new Vtiger_Field();
$field5->name = 'locationstate';
$field5->label = 'Location State';
$field5->table = $module->basetable;
$field5->column = 'locationstate';
$field4->columntype = 'VARCHAR(255)';
$field5->uitype = 2;
$field5->typeofdata = 'V~O';
$block1->addField($field5);
```

14. Add the **Location Zip** field:

```
$field6 = new Vtiger_Field();
$field6->name = 'locationzip';
$field6->label = 'Location Zip';
$field6->table = $module->basetable;
$field6->column = 'locationzip';
$field6->uitype = 2;
$field6->typeofdata = 'V~O';
$block1->addField($field6);
```

15. Add common vtiger fields such as **Assigned To**, **Created Time**, and **Modified Time**:

```
$field7 = new Vtiger_Field();
$field7->name = 'assigned_user_id';
$field7->label = 'Assigned To';
$field7->table = $module->basetable;
$field7->column = 'assigned_user_id';
$field7->table = 'vtiger_crmentity';
$field7->column = 'smownerid';
$field7->uitype = 53;
$field7->typeofdata = 'V~M';
$block1->addField($field7);

$field8 = new Vtiger_Field();
$field8->name = 'createdtime';
$field8->label= 'Created Time';
$field8->table = 'vtiger_crmentity';
$field8->column = 'createdtime';
$field8->uitype = 70;
$field8->typeofdata = 'T~O';
$field8->displaytype= 2;
$block1->addField($field8);

$field9 = new Vtiger_Field();
$field9->name = 'ModifiedTime';
$field9->label= 'Modified Time';
$field9->table = 'vtiger_crmentity';
$field9->column = 'modifiedtime';
$field9->uitype = 70;
$field9->typeofdata = 'T~O';
$field9->displaytype= 2;
$block1->addField($field9);
```

Now let's add some related fields. vtiger uses related fields to show one-to-one relationships between entities as well as one-to-many and many-to-one, such as contacts and accounts. These fields will show in the basic information section, along with the previous fields. We'll add a related account field, so as to know which customer this location belongs to:

```
$field11 = new Vtiger_Field();
$field11->name = 'relatedaccount';
$field11->label= 'Related Account';
$field11->table = 'vtiger_location';
$field11->column = 'relatedaccount';
$field11->columntype = 'VARCHAR(100)';
$field11->uitype = 10;
$field11->typeofdata = 'V~O';
$field11->helpinfo = 'Relate to an existing account';
$block1->addField($field11);
$field11->setRelatedModules(Array('Accounts'));
```

1. Now let's create a default filter, or view, for our module. It will just show all records:

```
$filter1 = new Vtiger_Filter();
$filter1->name = 'All';
$filter1->isdefault = true;
$module->addFilter($filter1);
```

2. Let's add some fields to the filter:

```
$filter1->addField($field1)->addField($field2,
1)->addField($field3, 2)->addField($field4, 3)->addField($field5,
4)->addField($field7, 5)->addField($field10,
6)->addField($field11, 7);
```

3. Now, let's say we want to see a list of multiple contacts under the record for a single location. We can associate multiple records of another module. Here's the code for associating multiple other contacts with this location. You can see that the code gives the user the ability to either add a new contact record while associating it with this location, or selecting a contact that's already in vtiger:

```
$module->setRelatedList(Vtiger_Module::getInstance('Contacts'),
'Contacts', Array('ADD','SELECT'));
```

4. Now, set the sharing access for the Locations module to Private. You'll be able to change it later in the **Settings** section:

```
$module->setDefaultSharing('Private');
```

5. Now, let's enable the Import/Export tool, but disable merging:

```
$module->enableTools(Array('Import', 'Export'));
$module->disableTools('Merge');
```

6. Finally, let's enable this module for use with web services:

```
$moduleInstance = Vtiger_Module::getInstance('Payslip');
$moduleInstance->initWebservice();
```

7. Close up the PHP file with some HTML:

```
echo '</body></html>';
?>
```

We've finished writing the code. Now, we have to save the PHP file we've created and move it into the root directory of our vtiger installation. Then we have to call it in our browser:

1. So, name the file `Create-Location-Module.php` and put it into the `vtigercrm` directory.

2. Go to your browser and type in: `http://<your-server-name>/vtigercrm/Create-Location-Module.php`.

You should see the following output in the browser:

```
Creating Module Location ... STARTED
Initializing module permissions ... DONE
Updating tabdata file ... DONE
Setting up sharing access options ... DONE
Creating Module Location ... DONE
Initializing webservices support ...DONE
Added to menu Sales ... DONE
Updating parent_tabdata file ... STARTED
Updating parent_tabdata file ... DONE
Creating Block LBL_LOCATION_INFORMATION ... DONE
Module language entry for LBL_LOCATION_INFORMATION ... CHECK
Creating Block LBL_CUSTOM_INFORMATION ... DONE
Module language entry for LBL_CUSTOM_INFORMATION ... CHECK
Creating Field locationname ... DONE
Module language mapping for Location Name ... CHECK
Setting entity identifier ... DONE
Creating Field locationaddress ... DONE
Module language mapping for Location Address ... CHECK
Creating Field locationaddress2 ... DONE
Module language mapping for Location Address 2 ... CHECK
Creating Field locationcity ... DONE
Module language mapping for Location City ... CHECK
Creating Field locationstate ... DONE
Module language mapping for Location State ... CHECK
```

```
Creating Field locationzip ... DONE
Module language mapping for Location Zip ... CHECK
Creating Field assigned_user_id ... DONE
Module language mapping for Assigned To ... CHECK
Creating Field createdtime ... DONE
Module language mapping for Created Time ... CHECK
Creating Field ModifiedTime ... DONE
Module language mapping for Modified Time ... CHECK
Creating Field relatedcontact ... DONE
Module language mapping for Related Contact ... CHECK
Setting relatedcontact relation with Contacts ... DONE
Creating Field relatedaccount ... DONE
Module language mapping for Related Account ... CHECK
Setting relatedaccount relation with Accounts ... DONE
Creating Filter All ... DONE
Setting Filter All to status [0] ... DONE
Adding locationname to All filter ... DONE
Adding locationaddress to All filter ... DONE
Adding locationaddress2 to All filter ... DONE
Adding locationcity to All filter ... DONE
Adding locationstate to All filter ... DONE
Adding assigned_user_id to All filter ... DONE
Adding relatedcontact to All filter ... DONE
Adding relatedaccount to All filter ... DONE
Setting relation with Contacts [ADD,SELECT] ... DONE
Recalculating sharing rules ... DONE
Enabling Import for Profile [1,2,3,4,] ... DONE
Enabling Export for Profile [1,2,3,4,] ... DONE
Disabling Merge for Profile [1,2,3,4,] ... DONE
```

If you take a look through the messages that vtlib shows you, you can see the various steps that it takes in order to create a module.

You can now keep your `Create-Location-Module.php` file in case you need to recreate your custom module.

Vtlib is a huge help in creating a custom module, since it saves a LOT of legwork. At the time of writing of this book, it did miss a few things on the creation of this module:

◆ It failed to create the `vtiger_location` table properly.

◆ It didn't create the `locationcity` column

◆ It didn't create the `locationzip` column

This caused an error when I tried to add a new record. I verified the table in the MySQL database. Once I created the two columns that were missing, everything worked perfectly.

By the time you try the above exercise, the vtiger team will probably have patched vtlib and you may not experience these issues. Just make sure to verify that the tables you've created with your script have been created properly. If you continue to have problems with your module, then use the vtiger log to see what's going on.

What just happened?

We just created a custom module successfully in vtiger. If you log in, you'll see the Locations module under the Sales menu.

We created the Locations module

By utilizing the power of vtlib and creating our own custom script that runs against it, we created the Locations module:

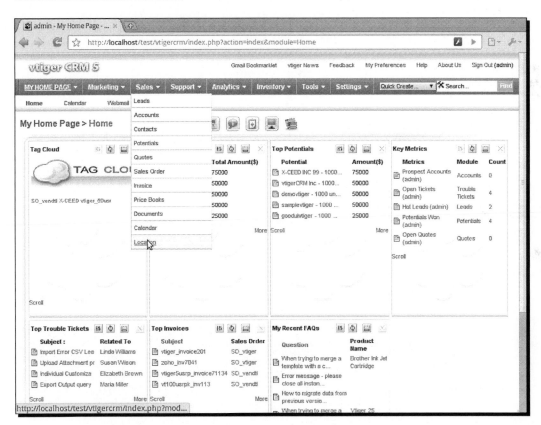

We added basic fields and the potential for custom fields

The Locations module has the basic address fields that we added and it has a related Account field:

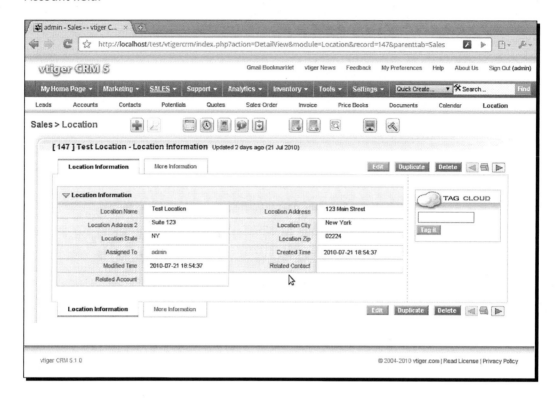

We added the ability to associate multiple contacts

On the **More Information** screen for a Location, you can see multiple related contacts at that location. You have the ability to create a new contact on the fly, or select one that's already in vtiger:

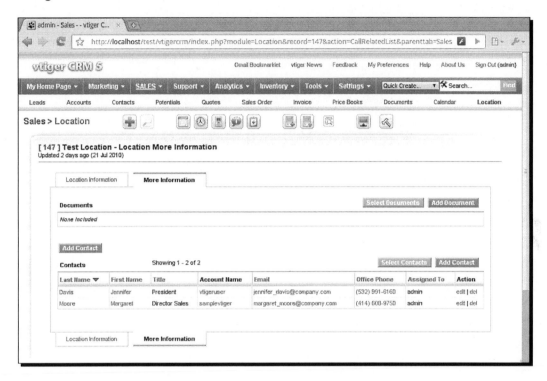

The locations module benefits from the entire vtiger framework

Since we've used vtlib to create this module, it benefits from the rest of the vtiger framework. It now appears in the **Settings** tool under **Sharing Access**:

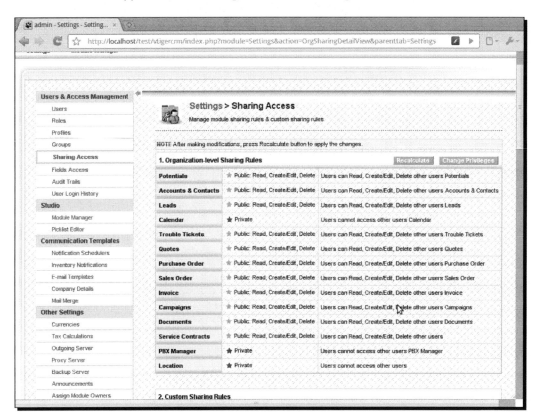

It can also now be used in Fields Access, Reporting, and so on. It's integrated into the vtiger environment.

Pop quiz – Creating a custom module

1. How do you:

   a. Write PHP code that will create and save a custom module when run against vtlib?

   b. Add fields to your new custom module using vtlib?

   c. Add related fields to your custom module (one-to-one relationships)?

Have a go hero – Doing more with custom modules

Now try adding other fields or related fields. Perhaps you could also try to add fields from the Products module that would perhaps show what Products a customer is using at a particular location.

Modifying your custom module further

Now that you've done all of the heavy lifting in creating your custom module, you can make some further modifications.

Let's say that you want to be able to:

1. See the related account and all related locations and contacts on the POTENTIALS screen.

2. Add a location or a contact from the POTENTIALS screen.

3. See all related locations, contacts, and potentials on the ACCOUNTS screen.

4. Add a location, a contact, or a potential from the ACCOUNTS screen.

5. See all related contacts, potentials, and the related account on the LOCATIONS screen.

6. Add a contact or a potential from the LOCATIONS screen.

It's fairly easy to do using vtlib once again. Here we go!

Time for action – modifying your Locations module

Let's create a new file called `Location-Mod.php` and stick it into your vtiger root directory (`vtigercrm` by default):

1. First, let's open the PHP file and turn on debugging:

```php
<?php
// Turn on debugging level
$Vtiger_Utils_Log = true;
```

2. Now let's include the necessary classes so we can modify the Locations module:

```php
include_once('vtlib/Vtiger/Menu.php');
include_once('vtlib/Vtiger/Module.php');
```

3. Now let's modify the **More Information** section of the **Location** screen to show a list of Potentials. The function `setRelatedList` takes as arguments the module instance that you want to link from (in this case, Locations), the label that you'll use in the listing of Potentials (Potentials), and the buttons to include on the listing (ADD and SELECT will allow you to add or select a Potential from the **Location** screen):

```
////////////// LOCATION SCREEN MODS

// Add the list of related OPPORTUNITIES to the Location screen
$locations=Vtiger_Module::getInstance('Location');
$locations->setRelatedList(Vtiger_Module::getInstance('Potentia
ls'), 'Potentials',Array('ADD','SELECT'));
```

4. Now we can modify the **Potential** screen to show the Locations that are related to it in the same way as we did in step 3:

```
////////////// POTENTIAL SCREEN MODS

// Add the list of related LOCATIONS to the Opportunities screen
// Only locations related to the account will be shown
$potentials=Vtiger_Module::getInstance('Potentials');
$potentials->setRelatedList(Vtiger_Module::getInstance('Location')
,'Locations',Array('ADD','SELECT'));
```

5. And we'll repeat this again to show a list of related Locations on the Accounts screen:

```
////////////// ACCOUNT SCREEN MODS

// Add the list of related LOCATIONS to the Accounts screen
$potentials=Vtiger_Module::getInstance('Accounts');
$potentials->setRelatedList(Vtiger_Module::getInstance('Location')
,'Locations',Array('ADD','SELECT'));
?>
```

6. Now just save the file as `Location-Mod.php` into your vtiger root directory.

7. Go to `http://localhost/vtigercrm/Location-Mod.php` in your browser (if vtigercrm is the name of your vtiger root directory) and you should see the following output:

```
Setting relation with Potentials [ADD,SELECT] ... DONE
Setting relation with Location [ADD,SELECT] ... DONE
Setting relation with Location [ADD,SELECT] ... DONE
```

What just happened?

We just modified our Locations module and extended its functionality.

Potentials

See the related account and all related locations and contacts on the **POTENTIAL** screen.

Add a location or a contact from the **POTENTIAL** screen:

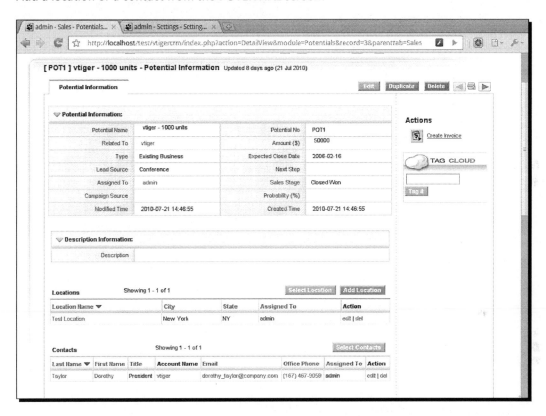

Accounts

See all related locations, contacts, and opportunities on the **ACCOUNT** screen.

Add a location, a contact, or an opportunity from the **ACCOUNT** screen:

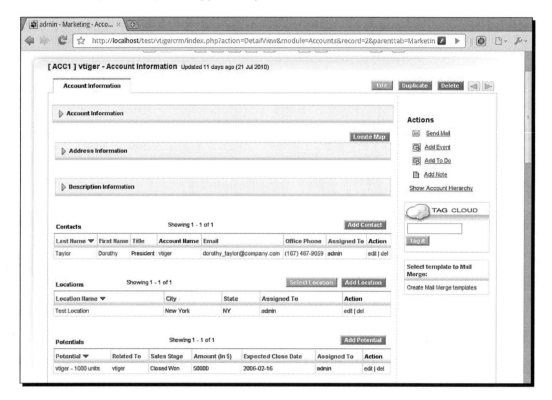

Locations

See all related contacts, opportunities, and the related account on the **LOCATION** screen.

Add a contact or an opportunity from the **LOCATION** screen:

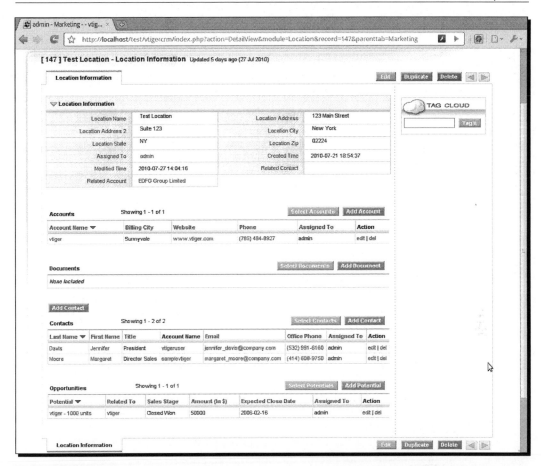

Pop quiz – Related fields in existing modules

1. How do you set a related list in existing modules utilizing vtlib?

Have a go hero – Create your own custom module

Now that we've created a Locations module with vtlib and integrated it with existing modules, try to create a custom module of your own that fits into your business model and then integrate it with the other modules.

Now that we've learned how to create custom modules, you've unlocked the true potential of vtiger. By harnessing the power of useful vtiger extensions, automated business processes and, now, custom modules, you're ready to run off into the wild and have your own adventures creating custom business solutions whether it is for your own organization or for your clients.

Managing you vtiger code over the long term

If you have made significant enhancements to the vtiger base code or have added custom modules to support your unique business model and processes, it is essential to protect that investment of time and money.

One way to do that is to use a **code version management** tool to backup and track your code changes. This has multiple benefits:

◆ In case of a disaster, you'll have a safe backup of your production code

◆ If you make enhancements that, for some reason, were not tested well before they were rolled into your production system, you can easily revert the changes

◆ Multiple developers can make contributions to the code

Subversion and Git

While an in-depth consideration of Subversion and Git are beyond the scope of this book, you would do well to consider using one of them to manage your code if your organization does adopt vtiger.

While subversion is self-dubbed as "a software versioning and a revision control system" and Git is self-dubbed as "a distributed revision control system", they both do very similar things—they allow you to control and manage versions of software code.

If you adopt these tools you will save yourself a lot of headache and also find that it can speed up your development efforts depending on how many people you have working on your project. (If you have more people the benefits increase.)

You can find more information about Subversion at `subversion.tigris.org`.

You can find more information about Git at `git-scm.com`.

I prefer Git's more modern approach. However, since Subversion has been around longer, there is an abundance off add-on tools that work with Subversion.

Using the cloud to support vtiger

There are two ways that you can use the cloud to support vtiger:

◆ Hosting your vtiger instance on a cloud server

◆ Hosting your vtiger system code in the cloud

Hosting vtiger CRM in the cloud

Among many others, a good cloud hosting provider like **The Rackspace Cloud** or **Amazon's EC2** can provide you with affordable and flexible cloud hosting. This takes the fuss out of managing your own hardware in-house and also gives your organization access to vtiger from anywhere else in the world. It will also allow you to scale up your vtiger system in size and power when you need it. Additionally, there are powerful and affordable backup options to keep your data safe. You can get more information by just Googling "cloud hosting" or checking out these links:

www.rackspacecloud.com

aws.amazon.com/ec2

Hosting your vtiger CRM system code in the cloud

As we mentioned, it would be wise to utilize a code version management system like Subversion or Git to manage your vtiger system code. Services like GitHub, Unfuddle, and Beanstalk allow you to do just that, but with a twist. You don't have to worry about keeping the code safe. They do that for you and much more. You can get more information by just Googling **subversion hosting** or **git hosting** or checking out these links:

www.github.com

www.unfuddle.com

www.beanstalkapp.com

Summary

By utilizing vtlib, which is a PHP helper library that allows us to quickly create custom modules with a short PHP script, we learned how to create our own custom module and integrate that module with the other core modules of vtiger—Accounts, Contacts, and Potentials.

Specifically, we covered:

- Creating a custom module
- Adding related fields to that module (adding a one-to-one relationship)
- Modifying existing modules to show several related records (adding a one-to-many relationship)

Now that you've learned the ins and outs of vtiger CRM, you have the power to significantly improve your organization's sales and customer service operations. However, as we say to our customers here at aimtheory: CRM is not a system, it is a mindset, an attitude, and an initiative. Make sure that as you set out on your endeavor to implement a CRM solution you have the backing up upper management and the cooperation of your staff.

If you implement vtiger CRM as described in the chapters of this book, you will be well on your way to CRM success. After that, dig deeper into your processes and see how you can further clarify and streamline them using custom fields, custom modules, and workflows. This will increase communication among your staff and, most importantly, between your organization and its customer—which is the key to success.

A
King of the Jungle—The Key to CRM Success

The important stuff first

This book is designed to make your vtiger project a success. However, I also want your CRM project to be a success. That requires more than vtiger. First things first. (If you want to get right into vtiger, skip to Chapter 2.)

CRM (Customer Relationship Management), as a concept, has been around for quite a while now. What does it mean? Well, for you, integrating a CRM tool most likely means integrating a CRM strategy or initiative within your organization.

Since the beginning of 2007, here at aimtheory (www.aimtheory.com), we had been trying to figure out how we could add real value in the CRM arena. It's a very highly competitive industry (almost $20 per click to get first place on AdWords) and there are new competitors entering the market every day. You've got loads of companies offering new products, companies claiming that they don't sell software (a.k.a. Salesforce) and app networks like Force.com and so on.

We gathered a few pilot customers and rolled out a robust, low-cost, open source hosted CRM service using vtiger. Throughout this pilot period, our goal was to work closely with our customers and prospective customers to understand their greatest challenges in implementing a CRM product. What we found was a huge surprise.

Our initial strategy was to compete with companies that charge per-user fees, because we firmly believe that the pricing model for most **SaaS (Software As A Service)** CRM solutions is unfair to the customer. While this message drew a lot of visitors to our site, we found a significantly different problem that our customers were facing.

The "what" of CRM

What do you see in the CRM market today? If you look at the CRM market today, you can see lots of companies touting their CRM tool over others, based on features and functionality. You even see some companies claiming that their tool is not software—even though it is a software in reality—as a differentiation strategy. In short, there is a whole lot of focus on *CRM tools*.

So, when I talk about "the what" of CRM, what is "the what"? Well, it's the tool. CRM software or web apps, or what have you.

In solving any problem, business or otherwise, the first thing you have to understand is the what. If you're solving a math problem, you first have to understand what you're dealing with. For example: "A train is traveling at 55 MPH...", you get the picture. This is the what of the problem.

Let's look at this now from the perspective of the CRM world. Long ago, the business world identified the "what" of the CRM problem. It became clear that sales professionals needed a tool to manage their customer relationships, sales activities and that it needed to gel with management's goals. Well, we've come a long way since then. We have a myriad of tools available that do exactly that, and a whole lot more that work with your accounting system, your iPhone, your iPad, integrate with Facebook, Twitter, Hoovers—you name it. The "what" is getting beaten into the ground.

Too many CEOs are trying to sit back and rake in the dough with the recurring revenue model of SaaS. Rhetorical: What value are their customers really reaping from that?

Anyway, just think about this—Will vtiger CRM, as a tool in and of itself, be the answer to your organization's CRM problem?

The "how" of CRM

During our startup phase, we began to ask customers, prospective customers, and CRM professionals this question: "What is the greatest challenge that you face in choosing/implementing/using CRM tools?" The overwhelming response really surprised us. We thought we had it pegged. We had lists of features ready that we wanted to add to vtiger CRM and plans for more integration with other tools and services.

The answer to our question was not even related to the CRM tool. The answer was: *user adoption/acceptance*.

Keep in mind, our focus group was comprised of individuals that used many different tools. We had some that used Microsoft CRM, Siebel, SageCRM, Salesforce.com, and more. Each of them said that their greatest challenge is getting their organization to buy into the idea of it and then getting their users to actually use the tool.

This changed the entire playing field and, therefore, our entire strategy. While our prepared feature lists still held some importance, we realized that it would be most important, from a business perspective and from our customers' perspective, to focus more on the "how" of CRM.

How to do the how

So then we sat down and asked each other, "How do we address this business problem—overcome buy-in issues and user adoption?" That may be a question that you've asked yourself before or you're starting to think about just now. That's when we started to focus more on offering CRM implementation services.

We found that many organizations reaped benefits from utilizing an external implementation team because we brought an objective, third party viewpoint to the table. In contrast with an internal team who may be managing multiple initiatives, we were able to give full focus and energy to the implementation. We could also lend our experience and expertise having performed many implementations previously—this usually resulted in a shorter implementation time.

So how can you be successful in implementing vtiger for the organization that you're working with? Will you have to have big meetings/lunches doing training and orientation and bang on management's door (with your head) to get help with sponsorship and enforcement of "the new system"? You may have a lot on your IT plate, so to speak.

Here are some principles that can help you to get your organization to adopt vtiger CRM as a tool to improve customer relationships.

Set the example

If you are in a position to influence others by your example, do it. This cannot be overstated. I'll never forget this skit that Ben Stiller did with Casey Kasem. This annoying guy with big sunglasses and a comb-over sees Casey Kasem in a restaurant on a date with his wife. He goes over to the table and insists that he do the voice from his radio show *American Top 40*. Casey tries to decline, but the Ben Stiller character just cuts him off and says, *N, n, na, na—do it*, in this low, Bronx-type lunk voice. Casey tries to decline again—*N, n, na, na—do it*. Over and over again, until Casey gives in. He even makes him do the voice of Shaggy from Scooby Doo.

This is what I'm saying to you: Do it. You will have an extremely difficult time getting other people in your organization (especially those that work under you) to adopt vtiger if you yourself don't use it. It doesn't mean that you have to set up your PC in plain sight of everyone in the office. Every email notification that they receive from vtiger for a new task or new lead assignment, and so on, will remind them that you're taking the lead in using the "new system".

Train and mentor users

"Give a man a fish and he'll eat for a day. Teach a man to fish and he'll eat for the rest of his life." A familiar adage for many of us. If we were to use this as an analogy for training and mentoring on vtiger CRM, it wouldn't mean that the training would be the 'teaching a man to fish' part. Rather, it would be giving the man the fish. More than training is required.

We can't expect to run through an hour, or even three hours of training, and then send the users off to happy vtiger land. We'll need to keep a connection with them throughout the course of the adoption phase and be available to answer questions and "show how".

If you're a team leader, make sure to do this with your team. *N, n, na, na—do it*. If you're not, encourage those who are team leaders to "'do it".

Get management to participate

If you are not the management and not influential, then you'll need to ally yourself with others to facilitate the adoption. If users get the feeling that using the new system is just a suggestion, then you know what that means—continued use of Post-It notes.

Do your best to encourage team leaders to:

1. Use vtiger CRM themselves and set the example.
2. Train and mentor their teams to use vtiger CRM.
3. Make their teams accountable.

It would be wise to set a specific length on the vtiger implementation project and set a cut-over date at which all users will start using vtiger CRM and stop using the old system (or Post-It notes).

Creating a CRM strategy

Now that we've nailed down the "how" of CRM, let's revisit the "what".

You've selected vtiger CRM and you're ready to go. Since you've gone through the motions of selecting a CRM package, you most likely have a CRM strategy in place. If you haven't yet developed a CRM strategy, read on.

A CRM strategy is at the core of CRM success, along with user adoption. A 2009 Forrester Research study found that 47 percent of CRM implementations fail, many due to a lack of CRM strategy and user adoption. Depending on the size of your organization, it can be a major undertaking. Since vtiger CRM is scalable to the enterprise, you may be faced with such an undertaking. While this isn't an exhaustive guide to CRM strategy, keep the following principles in mind when developing your CRM strategy.

Build your team

Having the right team is crucial. Start at the top—team leaders of the organization should be selected as key members. It would be very advantageous for the CRM project lead to be an external resource that has experience in CRM implementations. This will breathe energy into the entire effort as they will motivate other team members with their credibility and insight. He will be able to facilitate the creation of "the vision" and help stakeholders to agree upon what they want to do, why they want to do it and what exactly they want to improve.

All team members must be committed to the "the vision" of the CRM project and it would be helpful if they are politically influential as discussed earlier. All team members should work together to identify the business problem that vtiger CRM will eventually become the solution to.

Identify the business problem

Once the team has been assembled, they should work together to carefully identify the specific issues that the organization wants to solve. In other words, a business case should be made for the adoption of a CRM and how it will directly or indirectly improve the bottom line. If possible, scope out **ROI (Return On Investment)** projections. These should all be documented as they will eventually be used in a final project charter. The project charter will, in turn, be translated into requirements which will, in turn, be integrated into vtiger CRM.

Find the focus of the CRM strategy, whether it be customer service, marketing campaign management, sales order management, or sales force management and automation.

Identify IT requirements

This part of your CRM strategy is a necessary evil. The most important part being integration. Identify internal and external systems with which vtiger CRM will need to be integrated and develop a plan. You'll also need to look at your IT infrastructure and figure where vtiger CRM can fit into it or if you'll need to use a hosted service.

Set attainable goals

The team should also establish written, attainable project goals and adhere to them on a schedule. Each team member should be held accountable for the action items assigned to them. As one ancient writer put it, they should act "as men who must give an account". This will ensure the success and synergy of your team.

Phase the roll-out

In a profitable organization salespeople are busy making sales. Try not to overwhelm them with too much too fast. Plan to roll out vtiger CRM in stages, perhaps only starting with contact and calendar management. Then moving to lead management and so on. Continue this phased approach until you've reached all of the team's written goals.

In summary regarding your CRM strategy, the most important thing here is to make sure you give a careful thought to why you're implementing a CRM, what your expectations are for it, and how you'll accomplish it.

Summary

We learned a lot in this chapter about what to think about before you crack open vtiger.

Specifically, we covered:

- Why your CRM project is about much more than just the tool you've selected, vtiger CRM
- The importance of giving attention to your CRM strategy
- The need to have the right team and organizational support for your CRM project
- You figured out exactly why you want to implement a CRM before choosing and installing one

Whether you're reading this appendix before or after you've been through the rest of the book, don't forget these important principles. According to statistics, it can double the chances for the success of your CRM project.

B
Pop Quiz Answers

Chapter 1, Hello Kitty—What is vtiger CRM?

Question	Answer
1	C
2	C
3	D

Chapter 2, Unleashing the Beast—Installing vtiger

Question	Answer
1	B
2	A
3	C

Chapter 3, And the Claws Come Out—Getting Started with vtiger

Question	Answer
1	C
2	B
3	D

Chapter 8, Facing the Tiger—vtiger Theming

Question	Answer
1	C
2	B
3	B

Chapter 10, From Cub to King—Growing with vtiger

Creating a Custom Module

Question	Answer

1.A	```$module = new Vtiger_Module();```
	```$module->name = '[CUSTOM MODULE NAME HERE]';```
	```$module->save();```
	```$module->initWebservice();```

1.B	```$field1 = new Vtiger_Field();```
	```$field1->name = '[FIELD NAME]';```
	```$field1->label = '[FIELD LABEL]';```
	```$field1->table = $module->basetable;```
	```$field1->column = '[COLUMN NAME]';```
	```$field1->columntype = '[COL TYPE]'; //e.g. 'VARCHAR(255)'```
	```$field1->uitype = [UI TYPE]; //e.g. 1 for text field```
	```$field1->typeofdata = '[DATA TYPE]'; //e.g. E~M for a mandatory email field```
	```$block1->addField($field1);```

Question	Answer

1.C	```$field2 = new Vtiger_Field();```
	```$field2->name = '[FIELD NAME]';```
	```$field2->label = '[FIELD LABEL]';```
	```$field2->table = '[TABLE NAME]';```
	```$field2->column = '[COLUMN NAME]';```
	```$field2->columntype = '[COL TYPE]'; //e.g. 'VARCHAR(255)'```
	```$field2->uitype = 10; //Use 10 for related fields```
	```$field2->typeofdata = '[DATA TYPE]'; //e.g. V~M for a mandatory varchar field```
	```$field2->helpinfo = 'Relate to an existing account';```
	```$block1->addField($field2); //The block where the field will reside```
	```$field2->setRelatedModules(Array('Accounts')); //Indicate the related module```

Related fields in existing modules

Question	Answer
1	```$locations=Vtiger_Module::getInstance('Location');``` ```$locations->setRelatedList(Vtiger_Module::getInstance('Potentials'), 'Potentials',Array('ADD','SELECT'));```

Index

example 141
Introductory Call Reminder example 145, 151-154
Thank You note example 145-150
Workflow module
setting up, in Linux 144, 145
setting up, in Windows 142, 143
setting up, with third-party 142

X

XAMPP 24

Z

zend.ze1_compatibility_mode variable 25

Thank you for buying
vtiger CRM Beginner's Guide

About Packt Publishing

Packt, pronounced 'packed', published its first book "*Mastering phpMyAdmin for Effective MySQL Management*" in April 2004 and subsequently continued to specialize in publishing highly focused books on specific technologies and solutions.

Our books and publications share the experiences of your fellow IT professionals in adapting and customizing today's systems, applications, and frameworks. Our solution based books give you the knowledge and power to customize the software and technologies you're using to get the job done. Packt books are more specific and less general than the IT books you have seen in the past. Our unique business model allows us to bring you more focused information, giving you more of what you need to know, and less of what you don't.

Packt is a modern, yet unique publishing company, which focuses on producing quality, cutting-edge books for communities of developers, administrators, and newbies alike. For more information, please visit our website: www.packtpub.com.

About Packt Open Source

In 2010, Packt launched two new brands, Packt Open Source and Packt Enterprise, in order to continue its focus on specialization. This book is part of the Packt Open Source brand, home to books published on software built around Open Source licences, and offering information to anybody from advanced developers to budding web designers. The Open Source brand also runs Packt's Open Source Royalty Scheme, by which Packt gives a royalty to each Open Source project about whose software a book is sold.

Writing for Packt

We welcome all inquiries from people who are interested in authoring. Book proposals should be sent to author@packtpub.com. If your book idea is still at an early stage and you would like to discuss it first before writing a formal book proposal, contact us; one of our commissioning editors will get in touch with you.

We're not just looking for published authors; if you have strong technical skills but no writing experience, our experienced editors can help you develop a writing career, or simply get some additional reward for your expertise.

2136243R00132

Printed in Great Britain
by Amazon.co.uk, Ltd.,
Marston Gate.